FREIGHT (

Volume 3: Wales & Sc

A comprehensive guide to BR freight today by

Michael Rhodes & Paul Shannon

SILVER LINK PUBLISHING LTD

St Michael's-on-Wyre, Lancashire, PR3 OTG

CONTENTS

FRONT COVER: ABERCWMBOI Class 37 No. 37694 arrives at Abercwmboi with 6C57I, the SuO service from Severn Tunnel Junction, March 29 1987. The rake of empty HEA hoppers will be loaded with briquettes at the Phurnacite plant and the locomotive will return south with 6A021, a *Speedlink Coal* serice to Didcot. *MR.*

PREVIOUS PAGE: CAMERON BRIDGE: Class 20 No. 20227, resplendent in newly-applied *Railfreight* grey, shunts at Cameron Bridge on May 2 1986. The loco-motive had visited RNAD Crombie in the morning and now makes its second trip of the day from Thornton yard to Cameron Bridge. After depositing its load of two CO_2 tanks in the siding, the locomotive returned light to Thornton. *MR.*

REAR COVER, UPPER: MAESTEG: The character of the Welsh valleys is captured in this view of Class 37 No. 37693, arriving at Maesteg on May 31 1988. The train is the morning 'trip' from Margam TC. *MR.*

REAR COVER, LOWER: BLINDWELLS: On March 1 1988, Class 26 No. 26007 makes the short trip from Blindwells opencast site to Cockenzie power station. MR.

First published in the United Kingdom, November 1988.

Designed by Nigel Harris

Imagesetting by Ps&Qs, Liverpool, and printed in the UK by The Amadeus Press, Huddersfield, Yorkshire.

Rhodes, Michael, 1960-
    Freight only
    No. 3: Wales and Scotland
    1. Great Britain. Railway freight
    transport services: British Railfreight
    I. Title   II. Shannon, Paul
    385' . 24 ' 0941

ISBN 0-947971-28-9

INTRODUCTION

THIS is the third volume in a series of three books, and covers British Rail freight operations in Wales and Scotland. In the two years since *Volume One* appeared there have been major changes in the *Railfreight* infrastructure, particularly in South Wales. For example, sectorisation has led to a tightly-controlled allocation of motive power to different traffic flows and brought financial accountability to bear on all *Railfreight* operations. The responsibility for maintaining freight-only routes is borne nowadays by the freight sector which utilizes them. No longer do the costs of track renewal and resignalling come from the anonymous 'common purse'.

In South Wales the reorganisation of *Railfreight* has been dramatic. The 'hump' marshalling yards at both Margam and Severn Tunnel were closed in November 1987, and three smaller yards at East Usk, Cardiff Tidal and Margam Knuckle took over freight sorting in South Wales. The new yard at Margam contains just 18 roads and has direct access to the BSC works at Port

Left: **EAST USK: On July 12 1988, Class 37 No. 37009 storms out of East Usk Yard, past East Usk signalbox, with 6E64, the 1800 East Usk-Haverton Hill *Speedlink* service. MR.**

Talbot. The advantageous site of the sidings and increased block train working have meant that there is adequate capacity within the yard for a considerable expansion in *Railfreight* activity without the need for further sidings. Cardiff Tidal yard is a similar example of limited investment to provide facilities tailored to the Steel sector's needs. Here, 18 sidings handle the traffic from the Allied Steel and Wire factory, as well as steel services from Mossend and the North West.

Investment to provide modern lighting and strengthen the sidings was felt prudent, but lavish schemes like those of the 1955 modernisation plan are no longer justifiable. East Usk is the most striking example of the modern *Speedlink* philosophy. Just 11 sidings deal with all the wagonload traffic from South Wales, and careful timetabling and the minimum delay to wagons passing through the yard mean that there is always plenty of siding space to handle incoming traffic. No longer are British Rail yards used as large storage areas for goods in transit;

Above: Freight in the valleys. Class 37 No. 37693 arrives at Maesteg on May 31 1988 with a trip freight from Margam. *MR*.

rather they are now what they claim to be– sorting sidings where traffic is sorted as quickly as possible before onward transit to the customer.

Motive power and rolling stock are also continually changing. Older vacuum-fitted coal wagons have been displaced by air-braked HAA hoppers on all but the occasional train in South Wales. In July 1988, the input to Abercwmboi went over to HAA hoppers whilst in August, coal to BSC Margam benefitted from the construction of a new bottom-discharging reception point. Each *Railfreight* sector now chooses locomotives suitable for its freight traffic. The coal sector in South Wales has standardised on the Class 37/5 and 37/7 for trainload coal, but retains some Class 37/0 types for *Speedlink Coal*. By 1989, the *Railfreight* Metals sector will have standardized on the

Class 37 for all of its services. Both the Class 37/9 and 37/7 are used for this traffic.

In Scotland the story is very similar. Mossend yard, one of the busiest Traffic Centres in the country, is carefully monitored by one of the best organised TOPS offices in the country. Every foot of siding space is accounted for and earns its keep. There have been cutbacks, and investment by *Railfreight* in facilities suitable for the current traffic levels led to the closure of Craiginches yard in July 1988. The seven sidings at Guild Street are more than adequate to deal with the *Speedlink* freight around Aberdeen as long as wagons are not unduly detained in the yard.

The most striking advance in Scotland is the co-operation between *Railfreight* and the private sector in the distribution of goods. The old BR goods depots were dogged by two insoluble problems: restrictive practices and loss of goods. Enter the private sector. With active encouragement from *Railfreight*, the depots at Mossend (P.D. Stirling) and Deanside (J. G. Russell) were established. These now handle a vast range of products which might otherwise have been lost to the rail network.

Railfreight is now a profitable national transport system, showing much promise for the future. The Channel Tunnel is likely to further increase *Railfreight* activity and will hopefully lead to exciting developments in both motive power and marshalling yard construction. In the interim, *Railfreight* continues to build on its success in its 'core' areas of coal and steel transport.

In conclusion, we would like to thank all those who have helped with the *Freight Only* series as a whole. These include: Mark Bentley, Public Relations Officer (*Railfreight*) BRB, and Regional Freight Managers Andrew Nock, John Clarke, David Fletcher and Tony Smale, who were all kind enough to be interviewed during our research. In addition, David Clayton, Mike Hogg, Richard Phillips,

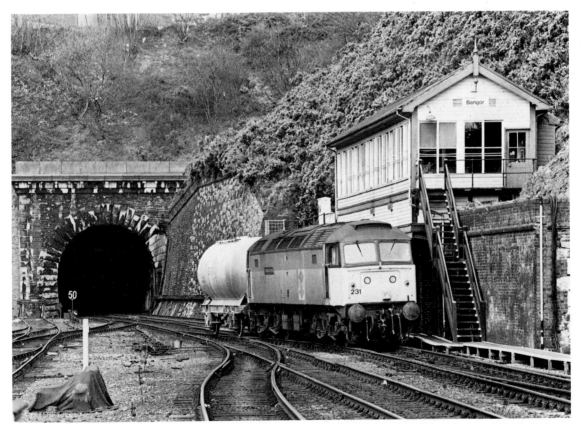

Above: On April 7 1988, Class 47 No. 47231 *The Silcock Express* **passes the signalbox at Bangor with a single empty Castle Cement tank wagon. PDS.**

Right: AYR: The 0948 'empties' from Ayr Harbour to Knockshinnoch (Falkland 'trip' R04) waits on the curve between Newton Junction and the site of Blackhouse Junction, whilst the driver's assistant collects the token for the single line section to Mauchline. The train is hauled by Class 20s Nos. 20192 and 20227, and the photograph was taken on July 13 1988. *PDS.*

Below: Class 26 No. 26014 arives at Millerhill Yard with 7G01, a *Speedlink* 'trip' from Methil Docks. Traffic includes empty Carbon Dioxide tanks returning from Cameron Bridge and an empty *Polybulk* wagon from Auchmuty. *MR.*

David Rapson, Ken Groundwater, Mike Welsh, B. Protheroe, Mike Cornick, Peter Kyrsta and Larry Fullwood all contributed to Freight Only Volumes Two and Three. Finally, special thanks are due to David Allen and Don Gatehouse who were able to fill in the photographic 'gaps' in Volume Three of the series. Our sincere thanks to them all.

Michael Rhodes,
Paul Shannon,
September 1988.

SECTION 1: WALES.

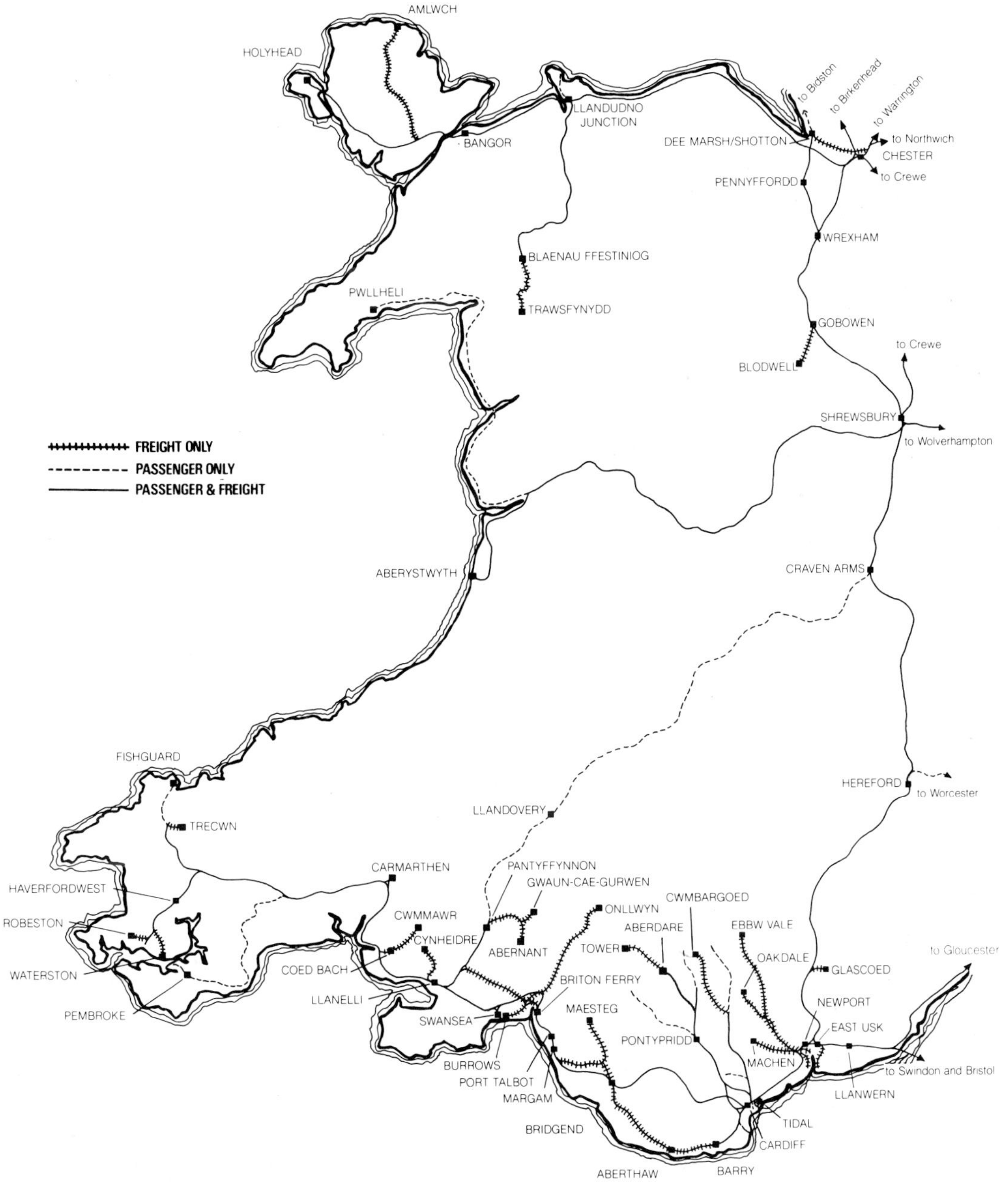

FREIGHT ONLY
PASSENGER ONLY
PASSENGER & FREIGHT

AMLWCH
HOLYHEAD
BANGOR
LLANDUDNO JUNCTION
DEE MARSH/SHOTTON
to Bidston
to Birkenhead
to Warrington
to Northwich
CHESTER
to Crewe
PENNYFFORDD
WREXHAM
BLAENAU FFESTINIOG
PWLLHELI
TRAWSFYNYDD
GOBOWEN
BLODWELL
to Crewe
SHREWSBURY
to Wolverhampton
ABERYSTWYTH
CRAVEN ARMS
FISHGUARD
HEREFORD
to Worcester
TRECWN
LLANDOVERY
CARMARTHEN
PANTYFFYNNON
GWAUN-CAE-GURWEN
CWMBARGOED
HAVERFORDWEST
CWMMAWR
ONLLWYN
ABERDARE
EBBW VALE
ROBESTON
CYNHEIDRE
ABERNANT
TOWER
OAKDALE
GLASCOED
to Gloucester
WATERSTON
COED BACH
BRITON FERRY
NEWPORT
PEMBROKE
LLANELLI
SWANSEA
MAESTEG
MACHEN
EAST USK
to Swindon and Bristol
BURROWS
PONTYPRIDD
LLANWERN
PORT TALBOT
MARGAM
TIDAL
CARDIFF
BRIDGEND
ABERTHAW
BARRY

THE SOUTH WALES MAIN LINE

MANY people first observe the freight traffic of South Wales from the window of the train as they speed along the South Wales main line between the Severn Tunnel and Swansea. A description of the freight terminals along the route, together with the pictures which accompany this section, will give flavour of the *Railfreight* activity in the area. For a detailed description of many of the railheads mentioned here, the reader should turn to the appropriate chapter.

Within seconds of leaving the Severn Tunnel, the traveller notices large areas of derelict sidings on both sides of the line. This is the site of the former Severn Tunnel Junction marshalling yard, which closed in November 1987. The yard was extensively modernised by the Western Region as part of the 1955 modernisation plan, and possessed both Up and Down shunting humps. These closed in 1978 and 1980, but the yard continued to function as one of 12 main *Speedlink* marshalling points. *Railfreight*

ABOVE: GAER JUNCTION: On July 6 1987, the afternoon Severn Tunnel-Cardiff Tidal yard *Speedlink* passes Gaer Junction. Class 37 No. 37223 is bringing empty wagons to Tidal, where they will be loaded with produce from the ASW plants in Cardiff docks. Since November 1987, this service runs from East Usk yard as 6B09, departing at 1438. In the background is a second Class 37 with a civil engineers train for Alexandra Dock Junction yard. The line to the eastern valleys climbs north behind the Tidal service. *MR.*

decided to close the yard which was inefficient for modern *Speedlink* traffic and from November 1987 all wagonload freight was diverted to other yards. Freight from the south west of England is now handled at Gloucester New Yard, whereas Cardiff Tidal yard and East Usk sidings now deal with South Wales *Speedlink* wagons. Three miles further west is the eastern exit from Llanwern steel works. This is followed a couple of minutes later by the western exit from the plant. As the train begins to slow at East Usk, the Uskmouth branch is seen on the left, followed by East Usk yard. *Speedlink* traffic for

The South Wales Main Line and its branches

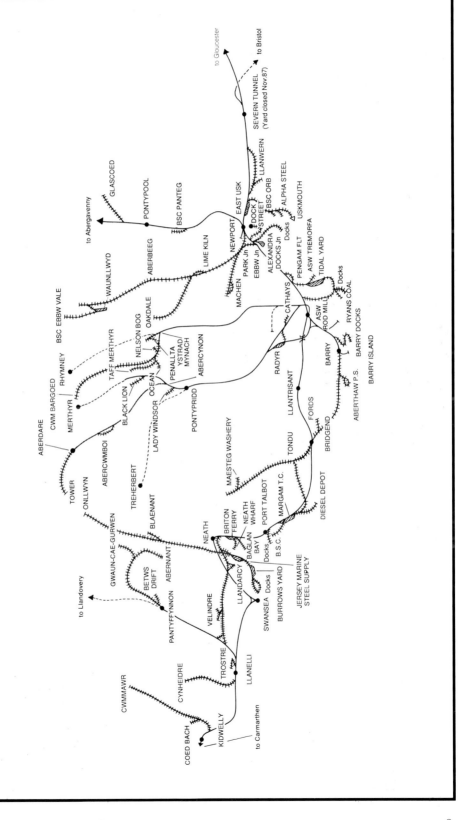

Right: UNDY: 6M87, the Severn Tunnel Junction -Carlisle *Speedlink* passes Undy, two miles west of Severn Tunnel, on July 9 1987. 47093 is hauling traffic from ASW in Cardiff loaded on BDA bogie bolsters, whilst china clay from Cornwall is carried in both PBA bogie tanks and Tullis four-wheeled vehicles. VDA and VGA vans carry a variety of commodities including government stores and timber. Although this service was cancelled with the closure of Severn Tunnel yard an afternoon freight still links South Wales with the North West and Scotland: 6S74, the 1645 Cardiff Tidal-Mossend service. *MR.*

the east and north east is handled here. Newport station is now the site for a locomotive stabling point (at Godfrey Road) where *Railfreight* motive power is parked at weekends.

Just west of Newport is the Hillfield Tunnel and then Gaer Junction, where traffic for Waunllwyd leaves the main line. Next come the sidings at Alexandra Dock Junction, where most of the engineering traffic in South Wales is marshalled. Opposite this yard is the shell of Ebbw Junction diesel depot, closed in 1985 when its work was transferred to Severn Tunnel Junction. Locomotive stabling subsequently returned to Newport Godfrey Road in 1987. The main line then runs south west, across the coastal mud flats until reaching the outskirts of Cardiff at Rumney. The first freight terminal is Pengam *Freightliner* depot on the south side of the line. From the western end of the depot, the branch to Tidal yard curves south. A second branch leaves for the docks at Windsor Bridge (Long Dyke Junction). This was the site of the general goods depot for Cardiff until 1980. A single track now winds through derelict ground to the ASW Rod Mill.

Departure from Cardiff Central is achieved passing Canton locomotive depot on the left and the Isis freight depot on the right. Ten miles along the Ely valley is Llantrisant, where branches up to Cwm and Coed Ely

diverge from the main line. These are both now closed, as is the Llanharan opencast site three miles further west, to the south of the line. Lack of planning permission for an extension to the Llanilid site, near Llanharan, led to the cessation of traffic from the loading point. The rail connection has been maintained, in case further opencasting starts in the area. At Bridgend the Vale of Glamorgan line joins from the south and the Tondu branch turns north from the mainline.

Water Street Junction, to the south of Margam yard, was removed in November 1987 when Margam New Yard closed. Hump shunting at the automated hump yard ended in 1979 and complete closure followed in 1987, after the completion of Margam Knuckle yard two miles further north. The Knuckle yard is correctly called Margam TC, or Traffic Centre. The Margam Abbey steelworks then stretches for three miles north, to Port Talbot station. A final three miles journey brings the traveller to Court Sart Junction where the Swansea avoiding line turns west. Baglan Bay chemicals works and Briton Ferry yard are seen to the left just before Court Sart Junction. From here to Swansea, there is usually no freight traffic along the main line, as all services from West Wales are routed via Morlais Junction and the Swansea avoiding line. Between Neath and Swansea the observer will notice two freight routes which pass under the mainline. The Neath Vale line to Onllwyn is seen 400 yards out of Neath station and then the Swansea avoiding line itself at Felin Fran. Arrival at Swansea is preceded by the sight of Landore shed to the right, half-a-mile north of High Street station.

Steel and coal traffic predominate along the mainline and a list of all freight services passing through Cardiff Central station is shown in the accompanying tables. These may carry up to a maximum of 200,000 tons of raw materials and finished goods within a busy 24 hour period! This represents the equivalent of *6000* lorries!

CARDIFF CENTRAL FREIGHT TRAFFIC (WESTBOUND) FROM AUGUST 1988

CODE	FROM	TO	TIME	TRAFFIC	DAYS
7C97	Taff Merthyr	Aberthaw	0056	MGR	MX Y
8B66	Alexandra Dock	Cardiff	0115	Departmental	MSX
6V23	Tunstead	Margam	0122	Limestone	WFO
7B23	Alexandra Dock	Trelewis	0233	Coal	SX
6B01	Didcot	Abercwmboi	0238	Speedlink Coal	MX
6B18	Cardiff Tidal	Margam	0238	Steel	MX
6B03	Didcot	Pantyffynnon	0326	Speedlink Coal	MX
7B94	Trelewis	Alexandra Dock	0348	Coal	MO
7B47	Cardiff Tidal	Pantyffynnon	0352	Coal	MX Y
7C76	Taff Merthyr	Aberthaw	0431	MGR	MX Y
7V30	Dagenham Dock	Swansea Burrows	0433	Speedlink	MX
6V26	Burn Naze	Barry Docks	0439	Chemicals	MWFO
6B02	East Usk	Bridgend Fords	0448	Speedlink	MX
6B23	Gloucester	Margam	0455	Steel	MO
6B51	Abercwmboi	Swansea Docks	0455	Coal	FO Y
6V88	Willesden Brent	Barry	0514	Speedlink	SO
7B54	Gloucester	Trecwn	0608	Speedlink	SX
6B34	Radyr	Onllwyn	0631	Speedlink Coal	TThO
6B26	East Usk	Trostre	0645	Speedlink	MX
7B36	Alexandra Dock	Llandeilo Junction	0648	Departmental	SX
7C78	Taff Merthyr	Aberthaw	0701	MGR	MX Y
7B24	Trelewis	Alexandra Dock	0703	Coal	SX
7B30	Alexandra Dock	Mill Pit or Maesteg	0714	Coal	SX Y
6B31	Llanwern	Port Talbot Docks	0853	Iron Ore	SX
6B06	East Usk	Barry	0858	Speedlink	SX
7C82	CwmBargoed or Penallta	Aberthaw	0901	MGR	SO Y
6V32	Albion (Gulf)	Waterston	0907	Oil	MX
7C82	Taff M or Deep Nav	Aberthaw	0915	MGR	SX
6B44	Stoke Gifford	Barry	0927	Speedlink	MSX
4B69	Pengam	Margam	0958	Freightliner	SXY
7B22	Hallen Marsh	Margam	1003	Coal	SX
7C83	Penallta	Aberthaw	1011	MGR	SX Y
4B84	Waunllwyd	Margam	1018	Steel	MO
6B10	Didcot PS	Margam	1022	Oil	SO Y
7V16	Grain	Margam	1031	Oil	MX
6B29	Swindon	Margam	1045	Steel	SX
7C84	Taff M or Deep Nav	Aberthaw	1111	MGR	SX
7B25	Alexandra Dock	Mill Pit or Maesteg	1113	Coal	SX Y
7C84	Tidal/Taff M/Deep Nav	Aberthaw	1126	MGR	SO Y
6B16	Radyr	Pantyffynnon	1201	Speedlink Coal	FO Y
6V87	Doncaster	Briton Ferry	1227	MGR	SO
6B40	Llanwern	Port Talbot	1235	Iron Ore	SX
7B66	Oakdale	Margam	1243	Coal	SX
6B14	Theale (Murco)	Robeston	1249	Oil	SO
6B38	Filton	Pantyffynnon	1310	Speedlink Coal	SX
7C85	Cardiff Tidal	Aberthaw	1312	MGR	SuX Y
7C85	Taff M or Deep Nav	Aberthaw	1312	MGR	SX Y
6B48	East Usk	Velindre	1259	Steel	SX
6V34	Albion (Gulf)	Waterston	1339	Oil	MTThSO
6V07	Ellesmere Port	Coedbach or Onllwyn	1401	Cawoods Coal	FSX
6V10	Ellesmere Port	Abercwmboi	1401	Cawoods Coal	FSO
6B16	Newport Dock Street	Pantyffynnon	1406	Speedlink Coal	MSX
7C86	CwmBargoed or Penallta	Aberthaw	1411	MGR	SO Y
6V05	Round Oak	Margam	1417	Steel	SX Y
7C86	Penallta	Aberthaw	1441	MGR	SX Y
6V89	Doncaster	Briton Ferry	1505	MGR	SO
7C87	Tidal/Taff M/Deep Nav	Aberthaw	1511	MGR	SO Y
6B08	Langley	Robeston	1520	Oil	TThSO
6B52	Llanwern	Port Talbot Docks	1535	Iron Ore	SX
7C87	Tidal/Taff M/Deep Nav	Aberthaw	1541	MGR	SX Y

Continued overleaf......

CARDIFF CENTRAL FREIGHT (WESTBOUND) Continued from page 11

6V65	Weaste or Ravenhead	Waterston or Robeston	1626	Oil	WFO
6V65	Glazebrook	Waterston	1626	Oil	MO
6V42	Dee Marsh	Margam	1632	Steel	SX Y
7C88	Cardiff Tidal	Aberthaw	1659	MGR	SX Y
6B47	Cardiff Tidal	Margam	1712	Steel	MO
6V43	Wednesbury	Margam	1712	Steel	MSX
8B05	Alexandra Dock	Llandeilo Junc	1722	Departmental	MO
7B80	Cardiff Tidal	Margam	1755	Coal	SX
9B27	Gloucester	Llandeilo Junc	1805	Departmental	TThO
7C89	Tidal/Taff M/Deep Nav	Aberthaw	1811	MGR	SX Y
7C89	Cwm Bargoed or Tidal	Aberthaw	1811	MGR	SO Y
6V39	Mossend	Margam	1826	Steel	SO
6B62	Llanwern	Llandarcy	1846	Oil	MThO Y
6B27	Theale (Murco)	Robeston	1851	Oil	SX
6B45	Exmouth Junc	Radyr	1900	Speedlink Coal	MWFO
7C90	Cardiff Tidal	Aberthaw	1913	MGR	SuX Y
7C91	Taff M/Deep N/ Penallta	Aberthaw	1913	MGR	SX
9B30	Alexandra Dock	Barry	1923	Departmental	SX
7B14	Heathfield (Gulf)	Waterston	1926	Oil	TO
6B60	Llanwern	Port Talbot Docks	1923	Iron Ore	SX
7B82	Marine	Margam	1926	Coal	FO
6B70	Taff M & Deep Nav	Radyr	1944	Coal	SX
6B58	Llanwern	Margam Abbey	1952	Steel	SX
6B56	Cardiff Tidal	Margam	2013	Steel	SX
7B91	Marine	Margam	2042	Coal	SX
7C92	Taff M or Deep Nav	Aberthaw	2043	MGR	SX
6V08	Eastleigh	Margam	2115	Steel	MO
6B67	Llanwern	Port Talbot Docks	2202	Iron Ore	SX
6B77	Llanwern	Margam	2224	Steel	SX
6V71	Partington	Baglan Bay	2239	Chemicals	MWFO
7C94	Penallta	Aberthaw	2241	MGR	SX Y
7B17	Cardiff Tidal	Margam	2253	Coal	SX
6V35	Ince (UKF)	Carmarthen	2252	Fertilizer	TO
7C96	Taff M or Deep Nav	Aberthaw	2341	MGR	SX
6V23	Tunstead	Margam	0005	Limestone	SuO

Right: EAST USK: A trainload of hot rolled coil (HRC) from Llanwern to Waunllwyd is seen approaching East Usk on March 3 1987. Class 37 No. 37903, a Metal Sector locomotive, is just half a mile into its journey with the 6A80 service. *MR.*

Above: LLANWERN : A special train of scrap metal passes Llanwern steelworks on July 7 1987. Class 20 Nos. 20142 and 20182 head the 7Z40 Snailwell-Tidal sidings service. The train has been staged at Whitemoor and Washwood Heath yards. *MR.*

Left: EBBW JUNCTION : The 6V67 Tees-Tidal service is a product of the closure of Follingsby Freightliner Terminal, in Newcastle. A major traffic from Follingsby was aluminium ingots for the British Alcan plant at Rogerstone. These were conveyed on pallets which were unloaded at Pengam terminal. After closure of Follingsby (in April 1987) a trial run of five FUA *Freightliner* vehicles commenced. These operated from the Lynemouth smelter to Tyne yard and then, after a crew change, on to Tees. From here, an overnight service delivered the wagons to Pengam and Tidal yard. The success of this experiment led to a regular service from Tees to Tidal using the Metals Sector locomotive to convey a variety of steel traffic to South Wales. In June 1988, new diagrams simplified the northern end of this operation with a Tees crew 'tripping' to Lynemouth in the afternoon to pick up the aluminium and bring it to Tees direct-ly. On July 8 1987, Class 37 No. 37217 passes Ebbw Junction with the Tees-Tidal service (which is without aluminium on this occasion) but still conveys only metals sector traffic. *MR.*

Right: MARGAM MOORS: An ideal train for the railway modeller is 6C16, the Panty-ffynnon-Radyr *Speedlink Coal* service which on July 10 1987 included just two HEA coal hoppers. Class 37 No. 37693 will take the coal, which is from Gwaun-cae-Gurwen, as far as Radyr, where a second 'trip' will return it to Swansea East Coal depot. The circuitous route was necessitated by the lack of a direct train from Pantyffynnon Swansea East. In 1988, the Gloda Coal Company (which operated Swansea East coal depot) went into receivership and this traffic therefore ceased, leaving Newport Dock Street as the only domestic coal depot in South Wales. *MR.*

Below: CANTON: Empty PTA iron ore tipplers return from Llanwern to Port Talbot docks. They are seen passing Canton on July 7 1987, in the charge of Class 56s Nos. 56031 and 56032, forming 6B40, the 1200 Llanwern-Port Talbot service. *MR.*

CARDIFF CENTRAL FREIGHT TRAFFIC (EASTBOUND) FROM AUGUST 1988

CODE	FROM	TO	TIME	TRAFFIC	DAYS
6M51	Waterston	Weaste	0010	Oil	WFO Y
6M51	Robeston	Ravenhead or Cowley	0010	Oil	WFO Y
6C76	Aberthaw	Taff Merthyr	0013	MGR	SX Y
6M78	Bridgend Fords	Edge Hill	0021	Speedlink	MX
6M10	Margam	Brierley Hill	0053	Steel	MSX
6B06	Margam	Barnwood Junc	0053	Speedlink	SO
6O08	Briton Ferry	Southampton	0058	Coal	SX Y
6M05	Pantyffynnon	Washwood Heath	0106	Speedlink Coal	MX
6M27	Waterston	Albion (Gulf)	0123	Oil	WFX
6M70	Baglan Bay	Partington	0150	Chemicals	MWFO
7B23	Alexandra Dock	Trelewis	0233	Coal	SX
6C05	Waterston	Heathfield	0237	Oil	TO
6A14	Robeston	Theale (Murco)	0251	Oil	SO
8B67	Cardiff	Alexandra Dock	0332	Departmental	MSX
6A08	Robeston	Langley	0358	Oil	TThSO
7B94	Trelewis	Alexandra Dock	0443	Coal	MO
6C82	Aberthaw	Taff M/Deep Nav/Pen	0453	MGR	SuX Y
6C12	Margam	Hallen Marsh	0517	Coal	SX
6B50	Radyr	Taff M/Deep Nav	0518	Coal	SX
7B31	Port Talbot Docks	Llanwern	0530	Iron Ore	SX
6B80	Margam	Waunllwyd	0548	Steel	MO Y
6C83	Aberthaw	Penallta	0555	MGR	SX Y
7B84	Radyr	Alexandra Dock	0615	Departmental	SX
6C34	Abercwmboi	Filton	0721	Speedlink Coal	MWFO
6C84	Aberthaw	Taff M/Deep N/Tidal	0730	MGR	SuX Y
7B24	Trelewis	Alexandra Dock	0805	Coal	SX
7B86	Margam	Oakdale	0817	Coal	SX
6A18	Robeston	Theale (Murco)	0838	Oil	SX
6C85	Aberthaw	Taff M/Deep N/Tidal	0840	MGR	SuX Y
7B40	Port Talbot Docks	Llanwern	0916	Iron Ore	SX
9B28	Llandeilo Junc	Gloucester	1011	Departmental	TThO
6A44	Margam	Swindon Cocklebury	1024	Steel	SX
6B41	Swansea Docks	Abercwmboi	1040	Coal	ThFO
6C86	Aberthaw	Penallta/Cwmbargoed	1040	MGR	SuX Y
6S43	Coedbach	Mossend	1100	Speedlink Coal	SO
6C87	Aberthaw	Cardiff Tidal	1106	MGR	SuX Y
6S60	Coedbach	Mossend	1112	Speedlink Coal	SO
6B28	Margam	Cardiff Tidal	1118	Steel	SX
6B17	Radyr	East Usk	1127	Speedlink	SX
6B58	Barry	Gloucester	1127	Speedlink	SX
6C87	Aberthaw	Taff M/Deep N/Cwm B	1140	MGR	SuX Y
7B52	Port Talbot Docks	Llanwern	1219	Iron Ore	SX
7B32	Mill Pit or Maesteg	Alexandra Dock	1220	Coal	SX Y
6C88	Aberthaw	Cardiff Tidal	1223	MGR	SX Y
6B78	Margam	Cardiff Tidal	1303	Steel	MO
6C89	Aberthaw	Taff M/Deep N/Tidal	1310	MGR	SuX Y
6C90	Aberthaw	Taff M/Deep N	1338	MGR	SO Y
6B45	Onllwyn	Abercwmboi	1343	Speedlink Coal	TThO
6B75	Margam	Llanwern	1353	Steel	SX Y
6B75	Margam	Llanwern or Tidal	1353	Steel	SX Y
8B51	Llandeilo Junc	Alexandra Dock	1423	Departmental	SX
6B66	Llandarcy	Llanwern	1413	Oil	MThO
4B96	Margam	Pengam	1426	Freightliner	SX Y
6C90	Aberthaw	Taff M/Deep N/Tidal	1427	MGR	SuX Y
6C91	Aberthaw	TaffM/Deep N/Pen	1508	MGR	SX Y
7B84	Radyr	Alexandra Dock	1525	Departmental	SX
8B60	Maesteg	Cardiff Tidal	1541	Coal	SX
7B60	Port Talbot Docks	Llanwern	1607	Iron Ore	SX
6C92	Aberthaw	Taff M/Deep N	1608	MGR	SX Y
6B94	Margam	Marine	1612	Coal	SX
7B26	Maesteg or Mill Pit	Alexandra Dock	1623	Coal	SX Y
6B19	Baglan Bay	East Usk	1645	Speedlink	SX
6B30	Barry	East Usk	1648	Speedlink	SX
6O84	Velindre	Dover	1654	Steel	SX
6C82	Aberthaw	Taff Merthyr	1824	MGR	SX Y
6C94	Aberthaw	Penallta	1841	MGR	SX Y
7B67	Port Talbot Docks	Llanwern	1853	Iron Ore	SX
6A35	Pantyffynnon	Didcot	1916	Speedlink Coal	SX
6C96	Aberthaw	Taff M/Deep N	1923	MGR	SX Y
6A01	Abercwmboi or Radyr	Didcot	2002	Speedlink Coal	SX
6B46	Margam	Cardiff Tidal	2008	Steel	SX
7B16	Coedbach	Cardiff Tidal	2018	Coal	SX Y

CARDIFF CENTRAL FREIGHT TRAFFIC (EASTBOUND) *Continued from page 15*

7B03	Carmarthen	Gloucester	2035	Speedlink	SX
6M66	Margam	Great Rocks Junc	2046	Limestone	MWFO
6O43	Llandarcy	Grain	2053	Oil	SX FO Y
6A40	Llandarcy	Didcot	2058	Oil	FO Y
6C97	Aberthaw	Taff Merthyr	2113	MGR	SX
6M22	Carmarthen	Ince (UKF)	2118	Fertilizer	WO
6L46	Swansea Burrows	Dagenham Dock	2202	Speedlink	SX
6M45	Barry Docks	Burn Naze (ICI)	2211	Chemicals	MWFO
6M18	Waterston	Albion (Gulf)	2223	Oil	SX
6L88	Trostre	Whitemoor	2243	Speedlink	SX
6B22	Margam	Waunllwyd	2253	Steel	SX
6M15	Onllwyn or Coedbach	Ellesmere Port	2305	Cawoods Coal	MSX Y
6M14	Abercwmboi	Ellesmere Port	2307	Cawoods Coal	MO
6M78	Bridgend (Fords)	Edge Hill	2323	Speedlink	SX
9B06	Margam	Alexandra Dock	2326	Departmental	MO

Below, left: LLANTRISANT : Class 47 No. 47217 approaches Llantrisant with 7C31, the 1020 Llanwern-Margam coil train. The HRC is bound for Trostre and Velindre and will be remarshalled at Margam yard. In 1988, this steel flow travels directly from Newport to the tinplate works at Swansea and Llanelli by means of the 6B26, 0618 East Usk-Trostre and the 6B48, 1235 East Usk-Velindre. *MR.*

Below, right: MARGAM: In the evening sun of July 10 1987, Class 56 No. 56052 coasts past Margam yard with 6C27, the Theale-Robeston empty oil train. Traffic from the West Wales refineries is detailed on page 67. *MR.*

Right: CANTON: On July 7 1987, the Margam-Severn Tunnel Junction *Speedlink* service (6A85) is seen passing the Isis Link depot at Canton. Class 47 No. 47051 heads a rake of BBA wagons, the last of which is the experimental covered version of this type of wagon. It is used for the carriage of finished steel, which requires protection from the elements. In the background are a line of Tiphook steel carrying vehicles loaded with steel from BSC Ravenscraig to BSC Orb works near Newport (see page 18) and BSC Lackenby to Tredegar Gas Pipes Ltd, near Cardiff. *MR.*

NEWPORT

NEWPORT is a prosperous town with a population of nearly 150,000. *Railfreight* activity in the town centres on the large British Steel works at Llanwern, where 45,000 tons of steel coil are produced each week. Both coal and iron ore are delivered to the works by rail. Coal is supplied by local pits at Oakdale and Marine and by Holditch colliery in Staffordshire. Coal from the north is delivered by the 7V56, 0254, MSX Basford Hall (Crewe) to Llanwern service. Some additional imported coal is also transferred from Port Talbot docks making the journey from Port Talbot's Margam yard by rail. This flow of traffic may form one limb of a new MGR rotation from August 1988 (see page 47). Iron ore travels directly from Port Talbot docks on what was once Britain's heaviest train, at 3300 tons. Haulage is by a pair of Class 56 locomotives, but (at the time of going to press) is to be changed to a pair of Class 37/7 engines with extra ballast to give greater adhesion for this heavy load.

Hot rolled coil (HRC) from Llanwern may be sent to several customers. Trainloads of coil may travel to BSC tin plating plants at Ebbw Vale, Velindre or Trostre. Cold reduced coil (CRC) may travel to the new finished

Above: LLANWERN: With BSC Llanwern in the background, Class 37 Nos. 37697 and 37889 wind out of the iron ore terminal with 6B52, the 1500 empty iron ore working to Port Talbot Docks. The week of July 21 1988 was the first in which pairs of Class 37/7s were tried on the iron-ore trains. At the time of going to press, it was planned to replace pairs of Class 56 locomotives with Class 37/7 locomotives by the end of 1988. *MR* .

steels terminal at Round Oak by way of 6M12, the 1230 Tidal-Wednesbury service, which calls here on its way north. Hot rolled coil is also sent to BSC Shotton on 6M47, the 0250 Llanwern-Dee Marsh service.

Since the closure of Severn Tunnel Junction yard in November 1987, the small collection of sidings at East Usk have taken a share of the *Speedlink* traffic dealt with at Severn Tunnel. The accompanying table details the arrivals and departures at the yard which has eleven roads ranging from over 100 SLUs to just 20 SLUs. The yard is often empty during the day – but this is a sign of efficiency rather than inactivity! Wagons spend as little time lying in the yard as possible and a combination of the site of the yard, well-trained staff, and an efficient timetable make sure that this is the case. A single Class 08 acts as yard pilot with a second locomotive responsible for 'trip' working from Llanwern. This changed in August 1988 with the introduction of two Class 09s to handle new traffic to BSC Panteg and BSC Orb.

A complex movement of stainless steel slab starts at SMAC in Sheffield, from where stainless steel slabs are shipped to Lackenby, Margam or Bremen via Goole and Grimsby docks. *Railfreight* is involved in all these journeys. Hot rolled stainless steel coil is then carried from these works by rail to BSC Panteg, via the yard at East Usk, from where a Class 09 'trips' the traffic twice each day. A second duty for the Class 09 is to the newly rail connected BSC Orb plant. Here, HRC from Ravenscraig is delivered for production into electrical steels. This is possible because of the installation of a 25-ton coil lift linking the railhead with the wharf. A second steel railhead on the branch is a private siding for scrap to the electric arc furnace at Alphasteel, which sees occasional traffic.

Steel is also exported via Newport docks. A fleet of SGW and SFW coil-carrying wagons are hired by BSC to carry coil to the docks from where trans-Atlantic shipping takes the product all over the world. Smaller ships dock at the Orb wharf. Tin plate may also travel to the docks in VAA and VBA wagons on an occasional basis. Timber imports at Newport are rail hauled to various customers around the UK. A large area of the docks has recently been taken over to provide a coal stocking and blending site. Here, coal from Trelewis and Maesteg may be blended with imported stocks before transfer by road across the Usk to Uskmouth power station, which lost its rail connection three years ago. Other occasional traffics which use the rail network in the docks comprise grain for export and coal from China, bound for Llanwern steel works.

The final railhead in Newport is the Dock Street coal depot, now the only domestic coal depot in South Wales. It is served by the

Above: **EAST USK YARD** became a *Speedlink* yard in November 1987, when Severn Tunnel Junction yard closed. On July 12 1988, yard pilot Class 08 No. 08493 is busy shunting wagons from the 6B42 arrival from Cardiff Tidal yard. On the right, Class 37 No. 37009 is at the head of the 6E64, the 1800 to Tees yard. The first two wagons in the train are empty HSA scrap carriers bound for Tinsley. Behind them are eight BDA steel wagons with ASW traffic bound for the Sheffield area. No. 47285 will head 6M92 (the 1928 to Willesden) which is being formed by the yard pilot. *MR*

6B07 service from Pantyffynnon via Radyr (MSX). The sidings at Alexandra Dock Junction may be used to stable this train before entering the branch but are mainly used as a base for civil engineering traffic in South Wales. Motive power for most of the *Railfreight* services in and around Newport is provided by the Godfrey Road stabling point, adjacent to High Street station.

EAST USK FREIGHT SERVICES (UP DIRECTION) FROM AUGUST 1988

CODE	DIRECTION	TO	ARR	DEP	TRAFFIC	DAYS
6M95	East Usk	Derby		0002	Speedlink	MX
6A36	East Usk	Swindon		0030	Speedlink	MSX
6V86	Warrington Arp	Stoke Gifford	0251	0354	Speedlink	MX
6A39	Cardiff Tidal	Westbury	0340	0410	Speedlink	SO
6O45	Cardiff Tidal	Hamworthy	0340	0410	Speedlink	MSX
6A36	East Usk	Swindon		0424	Speedlink	MO
4B84	Waunllwyd	Llanwern	0924	0950	Steel	SX
6E47	Cardiff Tidal	Tees	1132	1152	Steel	MX
6E44	Cardiff Tidal	Scunthorpe	1222	1247	Steel	MO Y
6B17	Radyr	East Usk	1155		Speedlink	SX
6B73	Hereford	East Usk	1558		Speedlink	SX
6B42	Cardiff Tidal	East Usk	1627		Speedlink	SX
6B19	Baglan Bay	East Usk	1709		Speedlink	SX
6B30	Barry	East Usk	1715		Speedlink	SX
6L91	East Usk	Dagenham		1750	Speedlink	SX
6E64	East Usk	Tees		1800	Speedlink	SX
6M92	East Usk	Willesden		1928	Speedlink	SX
7M83	Cardiff Tidal	Bescot	1945	2048	Speedlink	SX
7B03	Carmarthen	Gloucester	2102	2216	Speedlink	SX
6B83	Waunllwyd	Llanwern	2144	2209	Steel	SX
6L46	Swansea Burrows	Dagenham Dock	2230	0155	Speedlink	SX
6L88	Trostre	Whitemoor	2313	0025	Speedlink	SX
6M78	Bridgend	Edge Hill	2351	0045	Speedlink	SX

EAST USK FREIGHT SERVICES (DOWN DIRECTION) FROM AUGUST 1988

CODE	DIRECTION	TO	ARR	DEP	TRAFFIC	DAYS
6V80	Bescot	East Usk	0205		Speedlink	MX
6B35	Llanwern	Waunllwyd	0215	0247	Steel	SO
6V30	Dagenham Dock	Swansea Burrows	0255	0405	Speedlink	MX
6V06	Tinsley	East Usk	0322		Speedlink	MX
6V85	Whitemoor	East Usk	0352		Speedlink	MSX
6B02	East Usk	Bridgend		0420	Speedlink	MX
6V88	Willesden	Barry	0423	0450	Speedlink	SO
6V85	Whitemoor	East Usk	0446		Speedlink	SO
6B05	East Usk	Cardiff Tidal		0535	Speedlink	MSX
7B54	Gloucester	Trecwn	0509	0540	Speedlink	SX
6B05	East Usk	Cardiff Tidal		0550	Speedlink	SO
6B26	East Usk	Trostre		0618	Speedlink	MX
6B06	East Usk	Barry		0810	Speedlink	SX
6B15	Gloucester	Glascoed	0753	0819	Speedlink	SX
6V67	Tees	Cardiff Tidal	0800	0835	Steel	MX
6B51	East Usk	Moreton on Lugg		0900	Speedlink	SX
6V58	Scunthorpe	Cardiff Tidal	0855	0915	Steel	MO Y
6B88	Llanwern	Waunllwyd	1050	1115	Steel	SX
6B48	East Usk	Velindre		1235	Steel	SX
6B09	East Usk	Cardiff Tidal		1438	Speedlink	SX
6V99	Hamworthy	Cardiff Tidal	1950	2024	Speedlink	SX
6B59	Llanwern	East Usk	2324		Steel	SO
6V45	Willesden	East Usk	2337		Speedlink	SX

Left: NEWPORT DOCKS: In 1988, new rail flows of coal have started from Trelewis drift mine and Maesteg washery to Newport docks where coal is blended before a short road journey to Uskmouth power station. On July 12 1988, 08637 passes the customs offices in Newport docks with empty MDV wagons returning from the blending site to Alexandra Dock Junction yard. *MR.*

Above: ALEXANDRA DOCK JUNCTION: On July 6 1987, Class 37 No. 37142 passes Newport Alexandra Dock Junction with 6A44, the Margam Abbey-Swindon Cocklebury steel train. On the left, Class 37 No. 37222 stands in the sidings with 6C59, the Pantyffynnon-Dock Street Coal Depot *Speedlink Coal* train. On the right is the disused Ebbw Junction diesel depot. *MR.*

Right: NEWPORT DOCK STREET: The depot at Dock Street is the last domestic coal depot to remain rail-served in South Wales. Here Class 37 No. 37222 departs with 6B16, the 1325 *Speedlink Coal* service to Pantyffynnon on July 6 1987. The locomotive had just deposited seven HEA hoppers of household coal from Gwaun-cae-Gurwen in the sidings. *MR.*

NEWPORT VALLEYS

THE network of valley branch lines radiating north from Park Junction in Newport once boasted an hourly passenger service as well as numerous coal trains from more than two dozen pits. Rogerstone, two miles from Park Junction, was the site of a major hump marshalling yard which dealt with coal and steel traffic. In 1988, despite losses over the years, there are still heavy freight flows up the valleys to Ebbw Vale tinplate works and the collieries at Oakdale and Marine. British Railways also collect ballast from the quarry at Machen.

Waunllwyd is the exchange yard for BSC Ebbw Vale and receives up to five trains of steel coil each day. Hot rolled coil (HRC) may be delivered by rail from any of the three BSC plants at Ravenscraig, Llanwern or Margam. An output of approximately 300,000 tons of tin plate each year is for-warded by rail and road to the Metal Box company in the UK and also to customers abroad by way of the Dover train ferry or merchant shipping from Newport Docks and Orb wharf. Galvanised steel is also produced but this is distributed by road. The rail infrastructure at Waunllwyd will be completely renewed by the end of 1988 to make

Below: PARK JUNCTION: The branches from Machen and Waunllwyd converge at Park Junction, where they once connected with the lines to Ebbw Junction, Gaer Junction and Newport docks. In 1988, just the connections to Ebbw Junction and Gaer Junction remain. On June 23 1982 three Class 37 locomotives converge on the junction. Nearest the camera is No. 37295 with the 0A7O light engine working from Ebbw Junction to Machen quarry. Class 37 No. 37175 is pulling away with 6A83, the Llanwern-Oakdale coal 'empties' whilst 37227 waits for the road to Gaer Junction with 6A77, the Trethomas-Severn Tunnel Junction coal working. The coke works at Trethomas is now closed, as is Severn Tunnel yard. *MR.*

Right: ABERBEEG was once a sizeable yard where coal from the many local pits was marshalled before dispatch down the valley to Newport. The remains of the yard can be seen on the left of the signal box. On July 7 1988, Class 37 No.37293 slows for a token exchange before proceeding north with 6B92, the Cardiff Tidal to Waunllwyd conditional service. It is also worthy of note that the train was running two hours ahead of schedule on this day. *MR.*

way for the 1992 Garden Festival. A new yard will be sited half-a-mile north of the current sidings, and access to the BSC plant will be via a series of run-round sidings.

Two railheads remain which forward coal from the Western valleys. Marine colliery, south of Ebbw Vale, was opened in 1890 and should produce 370,000 tons of coal per annum. In addition, coal from neighbouring

Above: MARINE: The winding gear of Marine colliery can be seen in the background as Class 37 No.37298 awaits departure with 7A73, the 1242 Marine Colliery-Llanwern service on April 1 1987. The train was loaded in about 45 minutes by a pair of mechanical excavators. *MR.*

Six Bells colliery is brought to the surface at Marine, adding 280,000 tons to the annual output. In 1988, the planned four trainloads

Left: LLANHILLIETH: The dramatic nature of the South Wales valleys railways is graphically illustrated by this view at Llanhillieth, south of Aberbeeg. In 1986, Class 37 No. 37217 winds down the valley at the head of a Marine Colliery-East Usk service. The coal is destined for Uskmouth power station, which no longer receives deliveries by rail, which has led to the establishment of a coal stocking site in Newport Docks, as described in the text accompanying this chapter. *MR.*

Wales. Trainloads of coal are forwarded to BSC steel producing works at Margam, Llanwern and Scunthorpe. Departure times are as follows: 7B63, 0740 to Llanwern; 7B66 (SX) 1112 to Margam; 7B81 (SX)1444 to Llanwern; 7E95 (SX)1820 to Scunthorpe and 7E16 (SX Y) 2205 to Scunthorpe. At the time of going to press, coal to Margam and Llanwern was carried in antiquated MDV wagons, but from the end of August 1988 a new discharge terminal at Margam was to enable high capacity HAA hoppers to be introduced on this service. A new terminal at Llanwern has also been built to allow HAA hoppers to discharge at this location.

The quarry at Machen is rail-served and usually despatches a single trainload of British Rail ballast each day. The train runs as 8B61, the 1000 departure to Alexandra Dock Junction yard. A second service may run in the afternoon at 1520 (8B63) if traffic levels justify its operation. During 1987, a second stone flow emanated from Machen. This was to Allington in Kent and departed at 1800 as the 6Z28 duty to Stoke Gifford yard where the train was remanned for its journey east. This extra traffic was generated because of alterations to the ARC quarry at Whatley and is an example of the flexibility of *Railfreight* to respond to short-term policy changes by customers, always providing that several of their terminals are rail-connected.

each day to Llanwern or Margam steelworks has not been realised because of faults in the coal seams at the pits. British Coal are optimistic that production will return to full capacity by 1989.

The second coal loading point is at Oakdale. Dating back to 1908, this pit was extensively modernised between 1979 and 1985. Underground roadways link with Celynen North and Markham collieries. The annual output of 965,000 tons makes the Oakdale complex the most productive mine in South

WAUNLLWYD ARRIVALS, FROM AUGUST 1988			
CODE	ARR.	FROM	DAYS
6B95	02.53	Cardiff Tidal	MX
6B35	03.48	Llanwern	SO
6B82	06.17	Llanwern	MSX
6B80	07.05	Margam	MO Y
6B82	07.58	Llanwern/Tidal	MO Y
6B88	12.21	Llanwern	SX Y
6B92	16.59	Llanwern/Tidal	SX
6B93	18.50	Cardiff Tidal	SX
6B22	00.07	Margam	SX

Below: MACHEN QUARRY: In July 1987, stone was shipped from Machen to Allington in Kent. In this view, Class 56 No. 56056 is arriving at Machen with the 6Z28 service from Stoke Gifford, which brought the empty wagons from Allington to the quarry. *MR.*

Above: MACHEN QUARRY: On July 6 1987, a Rolls-Royce Sentinel diesel locomotive shunts BR ballast wagons which have arrived on the morning service from Severn Tunnel Junction. This traffic now travels from Alexandra Dock Junction yard. *MR.*

Below: OAKDALE: On April 1 1987, Class 37 No. 37899 draws under the rapid loader at Oakdale with 7A67, the 1140 Oakdale-East Usk coal train. Until October 1987, coal from the valleys north of Newport was staged at East Usk before final distribution to either Margam or Llanwern steel works. When East Usk became a *Speedlink* yard in November 1987, the coal was redirected by means of through services to the two BSC plants. Further modernisation implemented in August 1988 led to the introduction of air-braked HAA hoppers on services from Oakdale to the South Wales steel works. *MR.*

Left: WAUNLLWYD: The yard at Waunllwyd is due to disappear by the end of 1988 to make way for the 1992 Garden Festival, as described in the text accompanying this chapter. On April 1 1987, the yard contained BBA wagons loaded with steel coil from both Margam and Ravenscraig, with VDA vans awaiting departure with tin plate for Metal Box in Wisbech. Class 37 No. 37906 stands at the head of 4A85, to Llanwern, which is made up entirely of empty BBA wagons for Llanwern and Ravens-craig. *MR.*

NEWPORT – CRAVEN ARMS

Above: HEREFORD: On May 28 1985, Class 08 No.08491 shunts VGA vans containing palletised fertilizer. Other traffic in Hereford yard includes TTA tanks carrying bitumen from Ellesmere Port, and BDA bogie bolsters carrying special steel beams from Skinningrove, in Cleveland. *MR.*

THE line north from Newport was once a premier express passenger route, but in 1988 forms part of the secondary Provincial network. As well as regular trains from Cardiff to Liverpool, Manchester and Crewe, the line carries a considerable volume of freight traffic. The August 1988 timetable for the line is included in the Shrewsbury section of this book (page 69 & 70). The core commodities of steel, coal and oil form the backbone of services along the route but additional *Speedlink* services visit three locations along the line. At Moreton on Lugg and Glascoed there are large government stores depots and these are visited by: 6B15 (0720, SX) Gloucester to Glascoed service and 6B51 (0900, SX) East Usk to Moreton on Lugg freight. The second train may also pick up traffic from the busy goods yard at Hereford.

Hereford is also serviced by passing *Speedlink* trains. In the Up direction the 6S74 (1645, SX) Tidal-Mossend train calls between 1820 and 1943. In the Down direction both 6V86, (2150, MX) Warrington to Tidal (0118 to 0140) and 6V46 (0440, MSX)

Warrington to Tidal (0808 to 0914) call at Hereford. The yard handles general merchandise such as palletised fertilizer. In recent years timber has become an important traffic with OTA wagons being unloaded for two local customers. Bitumen from Ellesmere Port is delivered to Colas Bitumen Ltd, whilst the local Bulmer cider factory sends much of its produce north to Scotland by rail. Indeed, both Taunton and Bulmer cider arrives in Glasgow by rail.

The final *Railfreight* location along this line is the BSC plant at Panteg, just north of Newport. October 1988 witnessed the reintroduction of a freight service to this location and the details of this new service are described in the Newport section of this book (see page 18).

Left: GLASCOED: The 0720 (SX) Gloucester-Glascoed (6B15) eases along the Glascoed branch near Little Mill. On July 7 1988, Class 37 No. 37098 is heading a rake of VEA vans containing government stores. The first and last vehicles in the formation are VDA vans which are used as 'barrier' vehicles to protect the cargo from unexpected accidents. *Don Gatehouse.*

MORETON ON LUGG: On May 28 1985, Class 25 No. 25307 passes Moreton on Lugg signalbox with an extra freight from Ditton to Newport Alexandra Dock Junction yard. The train, coded 6Z68, conveys sleepers from the Ditton permanent way depot, for use in South Wales. *MR.*

Above: ABERGAVENNY: On April 5 1985, Class 47 No. 47069 is pictured passing Abergavenny with a special load of steel coil. The train is 6Z27 (Crewe-Severn Tunnel Junction) and conveys HRC from Ravenscraig to Ebbw Vale. The special working was needed because of locomotive failure on the previous day, which meant the regular Mossend-Severn Tunnel service had to be terminated at Crewe. *MR.*

Right: WOOFFERTON: Chemical traffic from Burn Naze to Barry and Partington to Baglan Bay traversed the 'north-west' route in 1988. An extra freight, 6Z70 from Heysham to Avonmouth (Severn Beach) is seen passing Woofferton signal cabin, on May 28 1985. Class 25 No. 25244 has five wagons of anhydrous ammonia in tow, separated from the locomotive by a barrier wagon. In the background is Clee Hill, the site of one of Britain's early warning installations. *MR.*

CARDIFF

CARDIFF, the capital of Wales, is a large and thriving city with a population of 285,000. The industrial heritage of what was once the world's largest coal-exporting port has been substantially erased as the city adopts its new role as a provincial capital. Since the closure of East Moors steel works and the run down of the docks during the 1970s, freight traffic in the city has fallen. In 1987 however, *Railfreight* increased its activity at the city's Tidal yard, after the closure of Severn Tunnel Junction yard.

Tidal Sidings are situated to the east of the city, in the dock area, and consist of 18 roads in the Tidal yard itself and a further ten shorter sidings in the Marshalling Sidings. In 1988, two new private sidings took over the western pair of roads in the Marshalling Sidings. One is owned by the Redland company, which receives bricks and tiles for distribution in South Wales, whilst the

Above: CARDIFF TIDAL SIDINGS: Tidal yard in Cardiff has seen a great upsurge in traffic since the closure of Severn Tunnel Junction yard in November 1987. In rainy weather on July 22 1988, Class 08 No.08836 draws forward with a train of steel billets from Scunthorpe, destined for Tremorfa works. Standing beyond is Class 08 No.08848, with wagons from the adjacent Redland private siding. The yard is heavily utilised, as can be seen from the large number of steel, scrap and coal wagons in the sidings. *MR*.

second handles hot rolled steel coil (HRC) en route from Ravenscraig to BSC's Orb works, in Newport. This traffic will be transported by rail directly to Orb works because *Railfreight* has won the contract, and the branch to Orb works from East Usk reopened in August 1988.

Flanking Tidal Yard to the east and west are the Allied Steel & Wire (ASW) factories. The Tremorfa plant is an electric arc furnace which consumes 1 million tons of scrap metal per annum. Most of this comes from

CARDIFF TIDAL YARD: ARRIVALS (EXCLUDING MGR SERVICES) FROM AUGUST 1988				
CODE	FROM	ARRIVAL TIME	TRAFFIC	DAYS
7B46	Pantyffynnon	0100	Coal	MX Y
6B98	Waunllwyd	0533	Steel	MX Y
6B05	East Usk	0610	Speedlink	MSX
6B05	East Usk	0624	Speedlink	SO
6V67	Tees	0945	Steel	MX
6V58	Scunthorpe	0950	Steel	MO Y
6B28	Margam	1200	Steel	SX
6V46	Warrington Arpley	1215	Steel	MX
6B78	Margam	1345	Steel	MO
6B75	Margam	1440	Steel	SX Y
6V43	Wednesbury	1414	Steel	MSX
6B09	East Usk	1515	Speedlink	SX
8B60	Maesteg	1618	Coal	SX
6V58	Scunthorpe	1633	Steel	MSX Y
6B57	Llanwern	1652	Steel	SX
6V75	Mossend	1832	Steel	SX (arr 1731 SO)
7V07	Washwood Heath	1915	Steel	SX
6B55	Swindon	2020	Speedlink	SX
6V99	Hamworthy	2058	Speedlink	SX
6B46	Margam	2050	Steel	SX
7B16	Coedbach	2115	Coal	SX
6V39	Mossend	2143	Steel	MSX
6V69	Wednesbury	2345	Steel	SX

Right: TIDAL BRANCH : Class 37 No. 37694 awaits clearance to enter the yard at Tidal, on July 1 1986. The train is 7A86, the Llanwern-Tidal service: this no longer runs in 1988. On either side of the line from Pengam are the earthworks of the old Roath branch, once used to deliver coal from the valleys directly to the docks and East Moors steel works. *MR.*

scrap merchants in the docks area, only one of whom is rail-connected. Indeed, there are no British Rail-connected scrap merchants in South Wales, but despite this handicap *Railfreight* delivers approximately 200,000 tons of scrap per annum to Tremorfa. This was carried in MDV and HTV wagons (see page 13) but the acquisition of 80 POA scrap wagons by Allied Steel & Wire has made this movement more efficient, as air-braked wagons can be incorporated into any *Speedlink* service and need not be formed into a block working as was the case with the older vacuum-fitted stock. The wagons have a distinctive black livery and have been nick-named 'Black-Adders.'

In addition to the scrap needed to produce steel rods and bars at ASW, there are also shipments of steel billets from Scunthorpe and Holland via Hamworthy docks. The output from Tremorfa and Castle works is used to reinforce concrete and sees distribution all over the UK as well as export via Cardiff docks. The accompanying photographs and table show how *Railfreight* has developed a series of freight services to deal with this traffic and now handles the lion's share of the ASW output, 100,000 tons of steel (about 10% of the ASW output) is exported from Cardiff docks and this travels over BR metals to reach the quayside at

Alexandra Dock. Imported timber is distributed via the *Speedlink* network in VGA vans (see page 31) and gas oil is regularly despatched from the Curran's terminal to Gower chemicals in Swansea (see page 54). Whilst steel, timber and oils are all railborne in the dock area, the largest rail user in the docks is still coal. Ryan's have a large coal stocking and blending site in the docks, which is rail linked. From here, blended coal is despatched via Tidal Sidings to Aberthaw power station. In future, it may be possible to run MGR coal services directly from the dockside facilities, thereby avoiding the costly tripping of coal to Tidal Yard.

Three Class 08 shunters work in the dock area. One is the yard pilot at Tidal, whilst a second engine acts as the Dock pilot. This locomotive is responsible for the transfer of traffic from the docks to Tidal yard and any cross-docks movements that may be necessary. A third engine is the Tidal 'tripper,' which serves the Isis link depot at Canton, the Redland depot at Tidal and the Ferry Road oil terminal (Sundays only). Isis is a *Speedlink* distribution depot with the emphasis on Metals sector traffic. Steel from BSC Lackenby (for local customers) is transhipped here from Tiphook wagons to local hauliers. Aluminium from Lochaber to British Alcan at Rogerstone is similarly transferred from rail to road. Like the Isis depot, Pengam *Freightliner* terminal relies heavily on the metals sector traffic for its revenue.

CARDIFF TIDAL YARD: DEPARTURES (EXCLUDING MGR SERVICES) FROM AUGUST 1988				
CODE	FROM	ARRIVAL	TRAFFIC	DAYS
6B95	Waunllwyd	0230	Steel	MX
6M40	Wednesbury	0115	Steel	MSX
6M44	Dee Marsh	0145	Steel	MX
6B18	Margam	0210	Steel	MX
6A39	Westbury	0305	Speedlink	SO
6O45	Hamworthy	0305	Speedlink	MSX
7B47	Pantyffynnon	0330	Coal	MX Y
6B82	Waunllwyd	0635	Steel	MO Y
6E47	Tees	1100	Steel	SuX
6E44	Scunthorpe	1150	Steel	MO Y
6M12	Wednesbury	1230	Steel	SX
6B92	Waunllwyd	1530	Steel	SX
6B42	East Usk	1555	Speedlink	SX
6V43	Margam	1630	Steel	SX (runs MO as 6B47)
6S74	Mossend	1645	Speedlink	SX
7B80	Margam	1705	Coal	SX
6B93	Waunllwyd	1720	Steel	SX
7M83	Bescot	1910	Speedlink	SX
6B56	Margam	1930	Steel	SX
6M46	Warrington Walton OJ	2000	Steel	SX
6E44	Scunthorpe	2040	Steel	MSX Y
6M07	Washwood Heath	2115	Steel	SX
7B17	Margam	2215	Coal	SX Y

Left: NORTH EAST JUNCTION: North East Junction was the entrance point to the dock network. The signalbox closed in the early 1980s, but the junction remains, controlled by hand points. On December 27 1985, Class 08 No. 08769 approaches the junction with a rake of HAA coal hoppers from Tidal yard bound for the A.J. Williams coal stocking and blending site. Here, they will be loaded with coal for Aberthaw power station, mixed with fuel imported from overseas. Output from the stocking site is larger during holiday periods and at weekends, when coal from South Wales pits is not available. *MR.*

Right: CARDIFF DOCKS Class 08 No. 08796 heads back towards Tidal yard with the evening trip from Currans Oils, on July 15 1988. The locomotive had delivered two empty VGA vans (in the background) for loading with timber and is seen leaving with a single VGA loaded with timber for Deanside Transit (see page 96). The two TUA tanks contain gas oil from Currans to Gower chemicals in Swansea. *MR*

Below: PENGAM: In evening sun on July 1 1986, Class 56 No. 56035 leaves the *Freightliner* terminal at Pengam with 4S8l, to Coatbridge *Freightliner* terminal. Only ten of the 25 FUA wagons travel through to Glasgow; the other 15 serve Manchester and LIverpool. *MR.*

Some general merchandise and occasional deep sea maritime containers are handled but aluminium from Lynemouth for Alcan at Rogerstone is the largest regular traffic. This travels south from Tees yard by 6V67, the 2350 Tees-Tidal sidings. The train calls at Pengam to detach *Freightliner* vehicles carrying the aluminium ingots. Aluminium coil returns north to Falkirk via Coatbridge on the 1830 Pengam-Coatbridge service (4S81). A second evening departure from Pengam is the 1754 to Stratford (4L70). The only other regular departure is 4B69, the 0950 to Margam. This is a conditional service known as the 'steel set' and links the large BSC plant at Port Talbot with the *Freightliner* network.

CARDIFF VALLEYS

Left: OCEAN AND TAFF MERTHYR JUNCTION: A classic image of the South Wales *Railfreight* business. With the winding gear of Deep Navigation mine in the background, Class 37s Nos. 37278 and 37898 negotiate the reverse curves as they head north to Taff Merthyr with a train of 'empties' from Cwm Bargoed (see also page 37) *MR.*

THE *Railfreight* presence in the valleys radiating north from Cardiff is for one purpose only: to move coal. Since the closure of Penderyn quarry, Dowlais iron works and Aberdare brick works in the early 1980s, there are no general freight customers left 'up the valleys'. Furthermore, the closure of the rail link between Aber and Taffs Well has left the rail network of the Rhymney valley completely separate from that of the Taff and Rhondda.

The Rhymney valley contains six rail connected collieries and opencast sites. At Cwm Bargoed there are two open-cast sites owned by Taylor Woodrow and Ryan's. The Ryan's site has been far more active in recent years and was used for blending coal from Trelewis drift mine until July 1987, (see page 37). In 1988, there are two conditional services each Saturday from Cwm Bargoed to Aberthaw power station. There are also booked weekday coal services from Deep Navigation and Taff Merthyr to Cwm Bargoed but these were not running at the time of writing.

Taff Merthyr and Trelewis collieries are

served by a single railhead at Taff Merthyr. Here, a rapid loading bunker is used to load up to 13 MGR services each day. In practice, only about six of these run, as other services are booked to serve either Deep Navigation, Penallta or Cardiff Tidal Yard. This arrangement allows freight services to be directed to whichever railhead has coal ready for collection. The pit at Taff Merthyr produces 582,000 tons of power station coal each year; all is used at Aberthaw power station.

Deep Navigation colliery lies just one mile south of the Taff Merthyr complex. It produces 587,000 tons of coal each year, mainly for the power station market. In addition to the MGR services (details of which can be found in the 'Cardiff Freight' table in the South Wales Main Line section) there are further coal and shale trains from the pit. Up to six trains each day shuttle between Deep Navigation or Taff Merthyr and Nelson Bog where shale from the pits is dumped. The

1855 Deep Navigation-Radyr (6B70) conveys *Speedlink* coal for the domestic market in HEA hoppers. A new service in 1988 is the 0510 Trelewis-Newport Alexandra Dock Junction Yard service (7B24). This coal is for blending in Newport docks and eventual transfer across the Usk (by road) to Uskmouth power station.

The final pit in the area is at Penallta. Opened in 1905, it was modernised in the 1950s and received a new high technology coal face in 1986. This produces 369,000 tons of coal each year, most of which is sent to Aberthaw power station in the three daily MGR services.

South of the Taff Gap lies Radyr. Here a large marshalling yard was built to handle coal from the Taff and Rhondda valleys. In 1988, the yard deals with both *Speedlink* coal and MGR traffic as well as departmental traffic and wagons from the nearby Cathays wagon works. The daily freight timetable is

RADYR FREIGHT TRAFFIC, FROM AUGUST 1988						
CODE	FROM	TO	ARR	DEP	PASS	DAYS
6C76	Aberthaw	Cwm Cynon			0020	MX Y
6M05	Pantyffynnon	Washwood Heath	0121	0246		MSX
6B01	Didcot	Abercwmboi	0251	0355		MX
6C78	Aberthaw	Cwm Cynon			0305	MX Y
7C76	Cwm Cynon	Aberthaw			0424	MX Y
7B94	Trelewis	Alexandra Dock	0401	0430		MSX Y RR
6B51	Abercwmboi	Swansea Docks			0441	FO Y
7B84	Radyr	Alexandra Dock		0600		SX
6B34	Abercwmboi	Onllwyn	0614	0707		TThO
6C34	Abercwmboi	Filton	0614	0707		MWFO
7C78	Cwm Cynon	Aberthaw			0712	MSX Y
7B24	Trelewis	Alexandra Dock	0717	0752		SX RR
6B07	Pantyffynnon	Newport Dock St	1002	1115		MSX
6B41	Swansea Docks	Abercwmboi			1101	ThFO Y
6B16	Radyr	Pantyffynnon		1130		FO Y
7B20	Coedbach/Onllwyn/Maesteg	Abercwmboi			1253	SX Y
6B17	Radyr	East Usk		1250		SX
6A01	Abercwmboi	Didcot	1316	1950		MO
6B45	Onllwyn	Abercwmboi	1404	1600		TThO
6V10	Ellesmere Port	Abercwmboi	1421	1423		FSO
8B51	Llandeilo Junc	Alexandra Dock	1450	1545		SX
9B67	Cathays	Radyr	1505			SX
7B21	Abercwmboi	Briton Ferry			1550	SX
9B68	Radyr	Cathays		1555		SX
6B05	Abercwmboi	Stoke Gifford	1630	1730		SuO
9B69	Cathays	Radyr	1750			SX
6A01	Abercwmboi	Didcot	1853	1950		TThO
6B45	Exmouth Junc	Radyr	1915			MWFO
6A01	Radyr	Didcot		1950		WFO
6B70	Deep Navigation	Radyr	1958			SX
6B41	Abercwmboi	Briton Ferry			2031	SuO
6M14	Abercwmboi	Ellesmere Port			2130	
7B33	Barry	Radyr	2157			SX
7B92	Alexandra Dock	Trelewis	2230	2255		SuO RR
6M14	Abercwmboi	Ellesmere Port	2240	2250		MO

Left: ABER: Aber is the site of the former junction for the line to Taffs Well. This closed in the early 1980s, effectively separating the rail network of the Rhymney valley from the other valley lines. On July 7 1986, Class 37s Nos. 37244 & 37308 head north with 6C91, the Aberthaw to Penallta colliery MGR service. The remains of the line to Taffs Well can be seen to the right of the train. *MR.*

Below: PENALLTA: On June 30 1982, Class 37s Nos. 37277 and 37288 await departure from Penallta colliery with 6O90 MGR service, which is due to leave at 1323 for Aberthaw. The train is loaded in two sections which are then joined for the journey south. This train still runs in 1988, but is re-coded 7C86 with a departure time of 1251. A single Class 37/7 is booked for the service nowadays, rather than the pair of unballasted locos shown here. *MR.*

shown in the table opposite.

Travelling north from Radyr the first large rail connected site was Nantgarw coke works. This closed with the consequent closure of its rail link on February 26 1988. At the time of writing, there were still several railway wagons in the works area but these are likely to be cut up 'on site'. Beyond Pontypridd lies the Lady Windsor pit, in Ynysybwl, which was producing 522,000 tons of coal a year during 1986/87. However, the pit closed early in 1988 because faults in the coal seams rendered it uneconomic. On April 12 1988, there was estimated to be 25 MGR trains worth of coal still to be moved from the pithead before closure of the branch from Stormstown, south of Abercynon. The final pit along the Merthyr branch is Merthyr Vale where 592 men produce 286,000 tons of coal annually. In February and March of

Below: NELSON & LLANCAIACH - On July 8 1987, Class 37 No.37284 passes Nelson & Llancaiach Junction with a train of spoil from Deep Navigation pit to Nelson Bog. Once it has passed, Class 37 Nos. 37898 & 37278 (right) will draw forward with their Cwm Bargoed-Taff Merthyr train, which will reverse for the last leg of its journey to Taff Merthyr. During 1987, coal from Trelewis drift mine was loaded into MDV wagons at Taff Merthyr pit for the journey up to A.J. Williams depot at Cwm Bargoed, where it was blended with opencast coal for eventual shipment to Aberthaw power station. *MR.*

Right: DEEP NAVIGATION: British Rail Class 08 No. 08202 was on loan to BC during July 1987, and is seen here at Deep Navigation coilliery. The HEA wagons in the background will be loaded with domestic coal to form the night 'trip' to Radyr yard (see table accompanying this chapter). *MR.*

Facing page, upper: TAFF MERTHYR: Class 37 No. 37895 has just run round its rake of empty HAA hoppers and is preparing to draw them forward through the rapid-loader at Taff Merthyr Colliery, on April 1 1987. The 1535 (7C89) to Aberthaw was running precisely on time. *MR.*

1988, major track alterations allowed BR access into the colliery avoiding the staging of coal in the colliery exchange sidings at Black Lion. One or two MGR services run each day to Abercwmboi Phurnacite plant.

The Aberdare branch has been much in the news, because of the planned reintroduction of a passenger service by October 1988. Freight traffic is buoyant on the branch. Coal for Aberthaw is loaded at Cwm Cynon as part of a scheme to clear large stocks of coal at Penrhiwceiber. North of Mountain Ash is

Below: See opposite page for caption.

Left: CWM BARGOED. High up above Merthyr Tydfil lies the A. J .Williams open-cast site at Cwm Bargoed. Until 1983, the branch continued a further 1 1/2 miles along the hilltop to Dowlais iron works but this section has now closed. On April 1 1987, Class 37s Nos. 37308 and 37275 shunt MDV wagons which have just delivered coal from Trelewis drift for blending. The best day to photograph the Cwm Bargoed branch is a Saturday, when there are usually three MGR services to Aberthaw. *MR.*

Right, upper: NANTGARW:
The branch to Nantgarw coke works closed on February 26 1988, leaving more than 100 wagons stranded at the works. These vehicles have since been scrapped on site. Here, on January 22 1985, Class 37 No. 37239 leaves with a 'trip' to Radyr yard. Lines of HUO hoppers which were formerly used to ship coke to Barry docks are stored out of use on the left. *MR.*

Right, lower: RADYR YARD:
On August 23 1985, Class 37 No 37223 leaves Radyr yard with 6C73, the Aberdare-Severn Tunnel Junction service. This was normally a through working from Abercwmboi to Severn Tunnel, with domestic coal from the Phurnacite plant but on Fridays also called at Radyr to pick up traffic. On this occasion the first six wagons are HEA hoppers with coal to Neasden, Letchworth, Watford and Fratton. The rear of the train is made up of wagons repaired at Powell Dyffryn works in Cathays. In 1988 the coal travels on the 6A01 service to Didcot (see accompanying table). *MR.*

the large Phurnacite plant at Aberaman, known by railwaymen as Abercwmboi because of the name of the signalbox which controls access to the site. Coal is delivered from Tower colliery as well as several other sites in South Wales including Merthyr Vale, Onllwyn and Maesteg. The output of the works is distributed widely in the UK via the *Speedlink Coal* network and also to Northern Ireland via Ellesmere Port (Cawoods) and Swansea Docks (Kelly's). Locomotives for the local MGR services to Tower colliery and Merthyr Vale are stabled at Aberdare station which is also host to the two Class 08 shunt-

ing engines which service Aberaman and Aberdare yard. High above Aberdare, on the heads of the valleys road, lies Tower colliery. The output of the last remaining Rhondda pit at Maerdy is brought to the surface here and the combined output of the two pits is 402,000 tons per annum. This travels to Abercwmboi in two daily MGR services comprising of 23 HAA wagons. There are also occasional trains of MDV wagons which carry coal to Ryans in Cardiff Docks where it is blended with the output of various other collieries for eventual use in Aberthaw power station.

Below: PONTYPRIDD: On July 8 1986, the Abercwmboi-Severn Tunnel Junction train (6C73) is seen passing Pontypridd. Class 37 No 37162 is in charge of a rake of HEA hoppers carrying domestic coal for depots all over Southern England. *MR.*

Left: ABERAMAN is the name of the Phurnacite plant at Abercwmboi, which is the name carried by the signal-box. Class 08 No.08350 is pictured shunting HTV hoppers in the yard at this location on March 26 1983. The wagons are bound for depots at Ratho, Kittybrewster, Inverness and Galashiels via Berwick. Although household coal is no longer handled at these destinations, there is a healthy tonnage of household coal still despatched by rail from Aberaman, for distribution to coal depots all over the country. In 1988, *Speedlink Coal* is responsible for this service. *MR.*

Left: MAERDY BRANCH: The last deep mine in the Rhondda Valley was at Maerdy. From July 1986, its coal was brought to the surface at Tower Pit, on the other side of the mountain. This led to closure of Maerdy Colliery in October 1986. Class 37 No. 37165 is pictured drifting down the branch with 7C70, to Abercwmboi. The coal was from surface stocks at Maerdy washery. In 1988, coal from the Maerdy seams is still delivered by BR to the Abercwmboi phurnacite plant, from the Tower colliery, in HAA hoppers (see below) *MR.*

Right: TOWER COLLIERY: On July 21 1988, Class 37 No. 37802 arrives at Tower Colliery with 7B69 from Abercwmboi. The 23 HAA hoppers will be loaded with coal for the Phurnacite plant. This locomotive and crew were based at Aberdare for the week with responsibility for delivering coal from Tower and Merthyr Vale collieries to Abercwmboi. *MR.*

Above: MERTHYR VALE: On October 19 1988, Class 37 No. 37796 arrives at Merthyr Vale pit with a rake of 20 HAA hoppers. The train is 6C72, from Abercwnboi, and will 'trip' coal to the Phurnacite plant at Aberaman twice in the day. Loading at Merthyr Vale is accomplished by a pair of 10-ton mechanical shovels, as seen here. Merthyr Vale pit is in the village of Aberfan, where a slag heap slipped down a hillside in 1967, engulfing the school and killing more than 100 children. *MR.*

Left: LADY WINDSOR: A short branch from Stormstown to Ynysybwl served Lady Windsor pit until May 1988. On July 8 1986, Nos. 37511 & 37508 are seen on the branch with 7C93, the 1620 Lady Windsor-Aberthaw MGR. This pair only had a short sojourn in South Wales before going to Thornaby for use on steel sector traffic. In January 1988, problems with the seams at Lady Windsor led to the decision to close the pit. The pit epitomises many of the problems of deep mines, which are an expensive and unpredictable way of producing coal. *MR*

41

Above: ABERCWMBOI: On March 29 1987, the SuO Abercwmboi-Ellesmere Port container train (6M14) leaves Abercwmboi, hauled by No. 37251. This was only the second week of operation for this train which comprised of 35 FPA containers loaded with domestic coal for the Irish market. Much of the export coal for Ireland had formerly been handled at Swansea docks, but investment at Ellesmere Port in a containerised system led to a change of port for this traffic. British Rail has, if anything, gained by the longer rail journeys involved! *MR.*

Above: ABERDARE: Class 37 No. 37694 stands in the remains of Aberdare station, on July 14 1988, with the 0730 Abercwmboi-Tower Colliery service (7B69). On the left is Class 08 No. 08664, one of two pilot locomotives which shunt at the Aberaman Phurnacite plant. The rake of MDV wagons will be loaded with coal for Tidal Yard in Cardiff, where it will be 'tripped' to A. J. Williams blending site in the docks. *MR.*

BARRY & ABERTHAW

Above: BARRY DOCKS BRANCH: Class 08 No. 08195 winds down into the dock area in Barry, on June 14 1982. The single Polybulk wagon had arrived on the morning trip from Severn Tunnel Junction. In 1988 this traffic reaches Barry via East Usk yard. *MR.*

BARRY, one of six rail-connected ports along the north bank of the Severn estuary, is also the train crew centre for South Wales MGR operations. The former steam depot is used to maintain the Welsh HAA fleet and stable the Class 37/7s responsible for MGR working to Aberthaw power station. The docks at Barry handle a number of rail-hauled commodities. Grain from East Anglia is exported with 25,000 tons a year arriving via the *Speedlink* service from Whitemoor to East Usk. The grain is then 'tripped' to Barry yard and taken on the final leg of its journey by the Class 08 pilot locomotive allocated to Barry. As one of a few MOD licencsed ports, Barry is able to export government stores, and occasional shipments of equipment arrive by rail. Chemical traffic also arrives in the dock area for the Dow works and BP's plant at Barry. Trains convey raw materials from Haverton Hill, Burn Naze (Fleetwood) and Baglan Bay. National Smokeless Fuels invested heavily in a rapid unloading plant at Barry with the aim of exporting coke from Nantgarw coke works via the port. A fleet of dedicated HUO hoppers were to be used on an MGR basis. Unfortunately, the facilities have never been used and stand derelict in the middle of Barry Cadoxton yard. A small amount of steel billet is imported for use by ASW in Cardiff and this is railed from the quayside to Tidal yard.

Aberthaw power station lies five miles west of Barry, on the coast. It consumes half of the annual output of the South Wales coalfield and is capable of burning up to 100,000 tons of coal each week. The pattern of MGR services varies from week to week, depending on the supply from different pits. A typical week in July 1988 saw the distribution as outlined in the table on page 44. Diagrams listed as 'To be announced' are those available to respond to day to day fluctuations in coal production at different pits.

Three further railheads exist along the Vale of Glamorgan line to Bridgend. The two Blue Circle cement works at Rhoose and

Right: ABERTHAW YARD: On March 30 1987, Class 37 No. 37898 departs from the yard at Aberthaw with the 6C88 working to Tidal yard in Cardiff. Aberthaw was particularly busy prior to the introduction of the Class 37/7 locomotives to South Wales, as each MGR required an engine change at this point. A pair of Class 37/0 engines were detached to allow a Class 47 with slow speed control to take the trainload of coal around the power station loop. The Class 37/7s have a slow speed control and this extra manoeuvre is therefore no longer required in 1988. *MR.*

Aberthaw no longer forward traffic by rail although it is to be hoped that *Railfreight* can regain a foothold in this traffic which is one of the 'core' commodities nationwide. Finally, the Ford works at Bridgend makes engines for various Ford vehicles and these are forwarded by *Speedlink* to the factories at Dagenham and Halewood.

MGR DISTRIBUTION FROM BARRY, JULY 1988 *(See also text on page 43)*			
CODE	**TIME FROM BARRY**	**TO**	**DAYS**
C77	0005	Blaenant	MX
C79	0145	Blaenant	MX
		Taff Merthyr	MO
C78	0230	Taff Merthyr	MSO
		To be announced	MSX
C82	0425	Taff Merthyr	FSX
		Cwm Bargoed	SO
C83	0420	Penallta	SX
		Steel Supply	SO
C84	0655	Ocean	MWO
		Maesteg	TThO
		Blaenant	FO
		Tidal	SO
C85	0805	Taff Merthyr	FSX
		Steel Supply	SO
C86	1010	Penallta	SX
		Cwm Bargoed	SO
C87	0950	Ocean	FSX
		Blaenant	FO
		Tidal	SO
C88	1155	Tidal	SX
C89	1310	Taff Merthyr	FSX
		Blaenant	FO
		Cwm Bargoed	SO
C91	1340	Penallta	SX
C90	1410	Tidal	SX
C92	1540	Ocean	FSX
		Blaenant	FO
C93	1655	To be announced	SX
Z94	1810	Taff Merthyr	FSX
C95	1930	Blaenant	SX
C96	1855	Taff Merthyr	FSX
C97	2120	Taff Merthyr	FSX
C98	2200	Blaenant	SX
Z76	2345	To be announced	SX

Right: ABERTHAW POWER STATION: No. 47230, fitted with slow-speed control, eases onto the power station loop at Aberthaw, on June 14 1982. In the background a pair of Class 37s can just be seen on another train. These will be detached to allow the second Class 47 pilot at Aberthaw to draw their MGR through the power station. During the late 1970's, trials were undertaken with a pair of Class 20 locomotives loaned from Scotland. These were found to be too light for the South Wales MGR work and in spite of their slow speed control were returned north within a couple of weeks. *MR.*

Left, upper: BARRY DOCKS: An unidentified Class 08 locomotive shunts on the quayside at Barry, on July 26 1986. The traffic comprises a single *Polybulk* wagon, containing grain from East Anglia. *MR.*

Left, lower: BARRY (DOW CHEMICALS): On July 26 1986, Class 08 No. 08795 is shunting at the Dow chemical plant. The morning trip from Cadoxton yard services the terminals at Dow, BP and the docks themselves. *MR.*

PORT TALBOT & VALLEYS

THE centre for *Railfreight* activity in this area is the new Margam Traffic Centre (TC). Here a collection of 18 double-ended sidings have replaced the sprawling and decaying remnants of Margam Hump yard, opened in 1960. The new layout allows access to the sidings from both the South Wales mainline and BSC Margam; indeed BSC shunting locomotives are allowed into the western section of the yard. Since opening in November 1987, there have been no real problems with accommodation at the yard. The key, in the words of the yard manager is to 'keep things fluid', by which he means that wagons are detained in the sidings for the minimum time. For the record, the last departure from Margam Hump yard was the 0925 Margam-Velindre coil train on November 1 1987, hauled by Class 56 No.56039. The first train

then entered Margam TC at 0600 (even though the connection with BSC Margam was not completed until 1300 on November 1 1987). The first train over this section was at 1305 on the same day!

The steel works in Margam produces 50,000 tons of steel each week, 95% of which is hot rolled coil (HRC). Rail input to the plant is in the form of coal and lime. Coal

Below: MARGAM TRAFFIC CENTRE - On May 31 1988, Margam Traffic Centre (built on the site of the former Margam Knuckle yard) has plenty of spare capacity for *Railfreight* traffic. Class 08s Nos. 08769 and 08897 shunt the yard whilst Class 37 No. 37255 stands at the head of the 6B28 departure for Cardiff Tidal yard. On the left, the rake of HTV hoppers has just arrived from Hallen Marsh behind Class 37 No. 37692, whilst the rake of MDV wagons on the right will form the morning departure to Maesteg. The South Wales Main Line is seen on the extreme right of the picture and BSC Margam is in the background. *MR.*

MARGAM KNUCKLE YARD ARRIVALS & DEPARTURES, FROM AUGUST 1988

CODE	FROM	TO	MARGAM ARR	DEP	TRAFIC	DAYS
6M10	Margam	Brierley Hill		0005	Steel	MSX
6B06	Margam	Gloucester		0005	Steel	SO
6B50	Velindre	Margam	0011		Steel	MX Y
6B49	Margam	Velindre		0205	Steel	SXY
6V23	Tunstead	Margam	0208		Limestone	WFO
6B18	Cardiff Tidal	Margam	0349		Steel	MX
6C12	Margam	Hallen Marsh		0420	Coal	SX
6B61	Velindre	Margam	0456		Steel	SX Y
6B80	Margam	Waunllwyd		0500	Steel	MO Y
8B46	Margam	Swansea Burrows	0535	0535	Steel	SX
6B23	Gloucester	Margam	0541		Steel	MO
6B21	Margam	Trostre/Velindre		0600	Steel	SX Y
7B86	Margam	Oakdale		0710	Coal	SX
6B26	East Usk	Trostre	0735	0815	Speedlink	MX
7B36	Alexandra Dock	Llandeilo Junc	0743	0845	Departmental	SX
9B28	Llandeilo Junc	Gloucester	0758	0905	Departmental	TThO
8B08	Briton Ferry	Margam	0828		Steel	SX
6B63	Velindre	Margam	0843		Steel	SX Y
6A44	Margam	Swindon		0920	Steel	SX
6B28	Margam	Cardiff Tidal		1030	Steel	MO
4B69	Pengam	Margam	1037		Freightliner	SX Y
7B22	Hallen Marsh	Margam	1051		Coal	SX
6B10	Didcot PS	Margam	1110		Oil	SO Y
4B84	Waunllwyd	Margam	1058		Steel	MO
7V16	Grain	Margam	1132		Oil	SX (SO Y)
6B29	Swindon	Margam	1137		Steel	SX
6B14	Margam	Llandarcy		1205	Speedlink	SX
6B78	Margam	Cardiff Tidal		1215	Steel	MO
6B75	Margam	Llanwern/Tidal		1305	Steel	SX Y
8B51	Llandeilo Junc	Alexandra Dock	1144	1310	Departmental	SX
4B96	Margam	Pengam		1345	Freightliner	SX Y
7B66	Oakdale	Margam	1357		Coal	SX
7B15	Margam	Coedbach		1355	Coal	SX Y
6B35	Trostre	Margam	1419		Steel	SX
6V05	Round Oak	Margam	1508		Steel	SX Y
6B94	Margam	Marine		1510	Coal	SX
8B09	Margam	Swansea Burrows		1558	Steel	SX
6B19	Baglan Bay	East Usk	1521	1600	Speedlink	SX
6B36	Margam	Trostre/Velindre	1625		Steel	SX Y
6V42	Dee Marsh	Margam	1712		Steel	SO
6V43	Wednesbury	Margam	1758		Steel	MSX
6B47	Cardiff Tidal	Margam	1758		Steel	MO
6B64	Velindre	Margam	1758		Steel	SX Y
7B80	Cardiff Tidal	Margam	1849		Coal	SX
6B46	Margam	Cardiff Tidal		1915	Steel	SX
6V39	Mossend	Margam	1917		Steel	SO
9B27	Gloucester	Llandeilo Junc	1943	1035	Departmental	TThO
6B64	Trostre	Margam	2000		Steel	SX Y
6M66	Margam	Great Rocks Junc		2005	Limestone	MWFO
7B82	Marine	Margam	2034		Coal	FO
6B56	Cardiff Tidal	Margam	2100		Steel	SX
7B91	Marine	Margam	2136		Coal	SX
6B44	Margam	Trostre/Velindre		2115	Steel	SX Y
6L88	Trostre	Whitemoor	2051	2138	Speedlink	SX
6B22	Margam	Waunllwyd		2150	Steel	SX
9B06	Margam	Alexandra Dock		2220	Departmental	MO
6B67	Llanwern	Port Talbot Docks	2243	2245	Iron Ore	SX (C)
6B77	Llanwern	Margam	2325		Steel	SX
7B17	Cardiff Tidal	Margam	2340		Coal	SX

from South Wales pits arrives in MDV wagons which are unloaded by a large wagon hoist in the BSC works. From August 1988, this will be replaced by a new bottom discharge shed which will allow HAA air-braked hoppers to be used. Limestone from Tunstead arrives three times each week by rail and is supplemented by road-hauled lime from Batscombe. Iron ore and some coal arrive at Port Talbot docks and are transported by conveyer belt directly to the blast furnaces. Rail has a major role to play in the transportation of HRC from Margam with wagons despatched each day to Shotton,

Right: MARGAM HUMP YARD: On May 31 1988, the hump yard is viewed from the hump top. The remnants of primary and secondary retarders are over-grown by weeds, as are the 50 sorting sidings. A sad sight. *MR.*

Trostre, Velindre and Ebbw Vale. In addition, cold reduced coil is sent to Swindon Cockle-bury yard for use in the Austin Rover auto-motive plant, Swindon. A spin-off traffic for *Railfreight* is coke, which is sent from the Grange coke works at BSC Margam, for use in the chemical works at Hallen Marsh, Bristol.

Above: PORT TALBOT DOCKS BRANCH : Class 56 Nos. 56041 & 56043 join the South Wales main line at Port Talbot Dock Junction with 6C52, the 1055 Port Talbot Docks-Llanwern iron ore service. Since 1982, when this picture was taken, there have been very few changes in the five or six daily services on this route. Towards the end of 1988, *Railfreight's* Metals sector aims to introduce pairs of Class 37/7 locomotives on this diagram. *MR.*

Left: MAESTEG: Coal is loaded by mechanical shovel at Maesteg washery, on May 31 1988. Class 37 No. 37693 is standing at the head of a rake of MDV wagons forming the morning service to Alexandra Dock Junction. The train conveys coal for blending in Newport docks. *MR.*

Right: MARGAM MOORS YARD: Three loops on the 'up' side of the South Wales mainline form Margam Moors yard. On July 10 1987, Class 47 No.47503 heads south with the 6A40 Llandarcy-Didcot power station (FO). The train was recessed in Moors yard to allow a crew change. In the background is Class 37 No.37162 at the head of the evening Trostre-Whitemoor *Speedlink* service. Crew changes now take place at Margam TC rather than at Margam Moors. *MR.*

Above: MARGAM ABBEY YARD: On July 10 1987, No. 47291 leaves the Abbey sidings at Margam. The Abbey yard was closed in November 1987 when Margam TC took over as both the BR yard and the main interchange point for BSC traffic. This train, 1945 (MWFO) Margam to Tunstead limestone 'empties' (6M66) ,has been rescheduled to depart from Margam TC since this date. *MR.*

Right: TONDU: No. 37701 arrives at Tondu with the 6C60 freight 'trip' of March 31 1987. This train ran from Margam to Maesteg and is seen here en-route from Maesteg to Cardiff Tidal yard with coal for blending. The last leg of the diagram wiil return the locomotive to Margam yard. *MR.*

Allied British Ports (ABP) operate the docks at Port Talbot. *Railfreight* views this as a single commodity port, the traffic being iron ore. There are five daily trains, each comprising 33 100 ton PTA tippler wagons. This timetable allows *Railfreight* to move just under 2 million tons of ore to Llanwern works each year.

Coal is still forwarded from two points in the area. Mill Pit is the rail loading point for coal from Park Slip opencast site. Shipments are made to both Cardiff and Newport docks for blending with other coals, before final delivery to Aberthaw power station. Maesteg Colliery closed in the early 1980s but continues to be rail served because of the large coal stocks still to be shifted from the site. The Maesteg washery cleans the coal before delivery to Abercwmboi phurnacite plant as well as Cardiff and Newport docks. In 1986 the stockpile was estimated to contain two

million tons of coal. Nearly three years later, and after two million tons of coal have been carried away from the washery by rail, there are still two million tons of coal remaining, according to the latest estimates!

The other two branch lines from Tondu to Wyndham and Garw pits were closed in 1985/86 but the line to Garw has been maintained in case the opportunity materialises to transport coal from the pit heaps at Garw.

Below: MARGAM MOORS EAST: The austerity signalbox at Margam Moors East still stands (at the time of going to press) at the southern exit from Margam TC, although it is now derelict. On July 10 1987, Class 47 No. 47342 passes the cabin with 6B09, the Briton Ferry-Margam Hump yard 'trip' working. The train returns empty steel wagons to Margam after they have delivered their cargoes to Neath Cargo Wharf. *MR.*

SWANSEA & VALLEYS

SWANSEA is Wales' second city, with a population of more than 150,000. The *Railfreight* presence in the area is based at two small marshalling yards, Briton Ferry and Swansea Burrows, with important local customers despatching a wide range of goods by rail.

Briton Ferry yard was designated as an overflow yard for *Speedlink* traffic when *Railfreight* was reorganised in South Wales, in November 1987. However, because of the success of the new Margam Knuckle yard, it has not been used in this capacity. Coal traffic to and from West Wales is often staged in the sidings and both Cawoods and Kelly's containers pause here on their way to Gwaun cae Gurwen, Cynheidre or Coed Bach. There are two weekend MGR services from Briton Ferry yard to Immingham. These depart at 1744 (7E87) and 2015 (7E89) on Sundays and convey coal from Cynheidre to the Petrofina plant at Immingham. Wagons of both HAA hopper type and the older MDV/HTV class may also be staged at Briton Ferry. Two local firms connect with the

Above: BRITON FERRY: On July 14 1988, Class 37 No.37268 approaches Briton Ferry with 6B19, the 1430 Baglan Bay-East Usk *Speedlink* service. The TTA tanks contain chemical traffic for Spondon and Saltend. *MR*.

Speedlink network via Briton Ferry. Highland Investments own the Neath Cargo Terminal, which lies at the end of a short branch from Briton Ferry yard. Around 30,000 tons of steel are exported each year to customers in western Europe and the USSR. Because of the tight curvature of the branch the standard BDA bogie bolster with disc brakes cannot be used for this traffic, and British Rail maintains a fleet of GWR-vintage and WR steel wagons especially for this freight flow.

Coal and chemicals are also dealt with at the Neath wharf, but these are mainly road-hauled to Neath. Just south of Neath on Swansea Bay is the Baglan Bay chemical plant owned by BP. Traffic for Saltend and Spondon departs on a daily *Speedlink* trip to East Usk yard, the 1430 departure (6B19). In addition there are block trains to Partington (6M70, 0010, MWFO) and Barry for Dow chemicals (6B11, 0500, TThO).

The second yard in the area lies at the entrance to Swansea docks, at Swansea Burrows. Not only traffic generated by the docks but also goods from Gower Chemicals freight depot and the nearby Ford plant are handled here. Gower Chemicals Ltd. own a general purpose freight depot built in the shell of the old steam locomotive depot at Danygraig. Regular consignments of chemi-

Below: NEATH CARGO TERMINAL: Dwarfed by the A48 dual carriageway bridge, No. 37250 reverses into the siding at Neath wharf. It arrived at Briton Ferry yard as 9C09, the Margam-Swansea Burrows 'trip'. On March 31 1987, there was no traffic from Swansea, so the locomotive simply picked up empty steel wagons from Neath and returned to Margam yard. *MR.*

Left: SWANSEA BURROWS YARD: Class 08 No. 08897 has just completed the formation of 6L46, the Dagenham Dock *Speedlink* duty. On July 20 1988, the train consisted of a single VGA van from Swansea to Barking, three OTA timber wagons carrying wood for Shotton, three empty TTA tanks for Avonmouth and a large rake of IPA ferry vans containing Ford traffic, bound for Dagenham. *MR.*

Right: SWANSEA DOCKS: The skyline here was formerly dominated by coal hoists which could bodily lift a loaded wagon and tip its cargo into waiting ships. These were dismantled in 1987, leaving a large area used nowadays to stockpile anthracite duff for export. No. 08896 is pictured on July 14 1988 drawing a rake of empty MDV wagons away from the quayside at Swansea Docks. *MR.*

Below: SWANSEA GOWER CHEMICALS: On March 31 1987, No. 08663 rolls into Burrows Yard with the afternoon 'trip' from Gower chemicals. The four empty TTA tanks will return to Avonmouth for another load of sulphuric acid. In the background is Llandarcy oil refinery. *MR.*

cals arrive from Avonmouth and Cardiff. Hopes of further traffic are high since the closure of the adjacent freightliner depot in 1987. Depots like Gower Chemicals may well act as local distribution centres for Channel Tunnel traffic after 1993. The Ford Motor Company manufactures axles and suspension units at their Swansea factory. These are sent to Dagenham on a daily *Speedlink* service, the 2050 Swansea Burrows-Dagenham Dock, coded 6L46.

Swansea Docks still flourishes, despite other industrial decline in the region, with a particularly bouyant export traffic of coal and steel. Four trains of domestic coal for the Irish market arrive each week from Coed

Left, upper: ONLLWYN: On 1 April 1987, a pair of British Coal locomotives bring coal into the washery at Onllwyn. The MCV mineral wagons have been sold by British Rail to the Coal Board and are used on internal traffic only. The NCB lettering can be seen in the lower leading corner of the first wagon, which contains coal from Banwen (Maesgwyn Cap). *MR.*

Left, lower: ONLLWYN: A train of household coal bound for Ireland is pictured on June 15 1982, leaving Onllwyn behind Class 37 No. 37232. The train was heading for Swansea docks, where the wagons were tipped into a waiting ship by the GWR coal hoists. Lack of container facilities at Swansea docks has led to the majority of Irish shipment coal being transferred to Ellesmere Port. *MR.*

Bach, Onllwyn or Abercwmboi. This makes a total of 2500 tons of coal arriving each week, in Kelly's containers, carried on FPA container wagons. Up to 6,000 tons of anthracite duff also arrives each week from Cynheidre and Coed Bach, and as this book went to press, deliveries from Gwaun-cae-Gurwen were due to restart in September 1988. This is exported to France and Morocco via the port.

Steel arrives from Margam in sheet form and Ebbw Vale as coils of tinplate for export

to Russia in large vessels. Smaller vessels dock at Neath as mentioned earlier. Occasional imports of hot rolled coil arrive from West Germany when production at UK plants cannot meet the demands of the principality's four tinplate and coating works.

Coal is produced in the valleys behind Swansea at Onllwyn and Blaenant. Onllwyn is an opencast disposal point, which collects coal from the nearby Maesgwyn Cap sites. A washery on site prepares coal which is then despatched by rail to a variety of customers.

Below: LLANDARCY: The complex plant and storage facilities of BP Llandarcy form the backdrop for this view on March 31 1987. Class 45 No. 45125 is reversing into the sidings with 6C14, the *Speedlink* trip from Margam yard. This working has since been reclassified 6B14 in 1988, but continues to depart from Margam at 1205. *MR.*

UK domestic coal departs in HEA hoppers twice each week to Radyr yard. Irish domestic coal leaves in Kelly's containers (for Swansea docks) or Cawoods vehicles (for Ellesmere Port). Vacuum-braked MDV wagons are also occasionally used for trainloads of coal to the phurnacite plant at Abercwmboi.

Activity at Onllwyn is dependent on stock levels in the surrounding opencast sites and

these were nearing exhaustion in 1988. Blaenant is a new drift mine, opened in 1976, and produces coal for Aberthaw power station. A staff of 640 men produce 512,000 tons of coal per annum. Because there is no washery at Blaenant, some coal must be shipped by road to Aberpergwm, in the adjacent valley, for washing. Sadly, the BR line to this pit closed in 1982, when coal production ceased, and has now been lifted. Most

Right: JERSEY MARINE STEEL SUPPLY: Class 37 No. 37301 runs round its train of coal 'empties' from Margam yard to Onllwyn, on December 2 1983. Jersey Marine Steel Supply sidings were used as a run-round facility for traffic at this time, and continue to be used by trains running to Blaenant and Onllwyn in 1988. *MR.*

Left: NEATH & BRECON JUNCTION: During a typical week in July 1988, there were 24 MGR departures from Blaenant Colliery to Aberthaw power station. On December 2 1983, Class 37 Nos. 37162 and 37300 pass Neath & Brecon Junction with the 7C93 service to Aberthaw. The train is classified as '7' because its maximum speed is 45mph when loaded. This MGR diagram continues to operate in 1988. *MR.*

Above: BLAENANT: On July 14 1988 the 1103 Onllwyn-Radyr (6B45, TTHO) *Speedlink Coal* service is seen passing Blaenant colliery. Class 37 No. 37227 is hauling four HEA hoppers containing household coal for the south of England. It is interesting to note that the train was two hours early at Blaenant. *MR.*

coal traffic from Onllwyn and Blaenant travels directly to customers in block loads. These must reverse in Jersey Marine Steel Supply sidings if they are to gain access to the South Wales mainline. A final occasional coal flow is from Brynlliw. There are still more than 200,000 tons of coal stockpiled at the closed pithead, and infrequent MGR trains are loaded on the Swansea avoiding line from where they take the coal to Aberthaw power station.

The Llandarcy oil refinery closed in 1987

but British Petroleum still produce lubricating and refined oils here. A regular *Speedlink* service leaves the works each day at 1330 for Margam (6B24). In addition, there are bulk loads of oils dispatched to Aberthaw, Llanwern, Didcot and Grain on an 'as required' basis.

The BSC tin plate works at Velindre works on a15-shift/week basis, producing mainly export tinplate. It is in many ways the overflow works, and as such possibly the most vulnerable to foreign competition. *Railfreight* plays a key role in keeping the plant competitive on the world market. Hot rolled coil is delivered from Margam, Llanwern or Ravenscraig (95% by rail). Finished coil may be sent to Margam on a *Speedlink* trip (see table) or dispatched on 6O84, the 1540 service to Dover, which connects with the train ferry and thus with European customers. It is hoped that such steel flows will increase when British Steel is privatised and the Channel Tunnel completed.

Below: VELINDRE: Seven ferry vans carrying tin-plated coil form the load for Class 47 No. 47359, as it stands in the exchange sidings at Velindre tin plate works on July 14 1988. The wagons are bound for Sosek Fabrike (in Belgrade) via the Dover train ferry, which will be reached directly via 6O84, the 1540 Velindre-Dover *Speedlink* service. Other traffic in the yard on this day included plated coil on BBA wagons, bound for Margam, and tinplate in VAB vans, destined for the Metal Box factory at Aintree. *MR.*

FREIGHT ONLY

LLANELLI

LLANELLI was once a centre for heavy industry and boasted a hump marshalling yard at Llandeilo Junction, one mile east of the town. Since the complete closure of Llandeilo Junction yard in 1982, *Railfreight* has remained active in the area with both local coal and steel gaining benefit from rail transportation. Trostre tinplate works receives HRC from Ravenscraig, Margam and Llanwern. It forwards tinplate by rail on the 2000 to Whitemoor (6L88) whilst HRC arrives on the 0205 from Margam (6B49, SX Y), the 0605 from Margam (6B21, SX Y), the 0618 from East Usk (6B26, MX), the 1625 from Margam (6B36, SX Y) and the 2115 from Margam (6B44, SX Y).

Coal is produced at Cynheidre colliery,

Above: LLANELLI: The 1604 Milford Haven-Margam *Speedlink* service (7C03) passes Llanelli on July 4 1986. In 1988, the traffic on this train runs on 7B57, the 1135 Trecwn-Gloucester *Speedlink* freight. Class 37 No. 37129 hauls a single OTA timber wagon, carrying wood for Shotton and five PCA cement tanks returning empty from Carmarthen to Aberthaw. This traffic no longer travels by rail as there is no cement traffic in South Wales in 1988. In the background are, from left to right, Class 08 No. 08191 (the Llanelli pilot), 08991 & 08992 (the Cwmmawr engines) and Class 37 No. 37227, awaiting an engineering turn. *MR.*

opened in 1939, and subsequently extended in 1986 with the introduction of coal production from the Carway Fawr drift mine. An annual output of 291,000 tons of anthracite is produced by the 794-strong work force. Anthracite duff travels by rail to

Swansea docks via 7B96, the 0840 (SX Y) departure from Cynheidre. The completion of new rapid-loading facilities in January 1988 has led to weekend MGR services to Immingham being introduced. This takes industrial fuel to the *Petrofina* oil refinery at Immingham.

Two opencast collection points exist at Cwmmawr and Coed Bach. Coal from the Ffos Las opencast scheme and other smaller projects is brought to these railheads by lorry and forwarded to household coal depots courtesy of the new *Speedlink Coal* network. A train crew from Pantyffynnon travels by

Above: TROSTRE: Class 56 No. 56038 arrives at Trostre with 6B44, the 2114 Margam-Trostre coil train. The train was one hour early, allowing a midsummer view on August 27 1982. *MR.*

taxi to Cwmmawr at lunchtime, to take the afternoon trip down to Coed Bach. They then return to Cwmmawr with their cut-down cab Class 08 and catch the taxi back to Panty-

Below: CYNHEIDRE: It took Class 37 No. 37258 nearly one hour to climb the five miles from Llanelli with its load of empties, because of wheel slip on the wet rails. The 9B86 service from Llanelli was loaded at Cynheidre with anthracite duff for Swansea docks on July 2 1987. *MR.*

Above, left: PONT NEWYDD: On July 3 1986, Class 08s Nos.08992 and 08991 wind down the Cwmmawr branch with the morning trip to Coed Bach. At this time, the locomotives were driven by train crews from Llanelli and hence stabled at Llanelli overnight. In 1988, the train crew depot at Llanelli was closed; the Cwmmawr trip has been retimed for the afternoon and is now worked by Pantyffynnon drivers. *MR.*

Above, right: KIDWELLY: Class 37 No.37181 takes the new connection from Coed Bach to Kidwelly, on July 4 1986, with 6C94, the Coed Bach-Severn Tunnel Junction service. This conveyed *Speedlink* coal which, in 1988, travels on the 6B55 service. *MR.*

ffynnon. The locomotive stables overnight at Cwmmawr. At Coed Bach, coal is washed and despatched in one of three ways. HEA hoppers of *Speedlink* coal leave on the 0840 to Mossend (6S43, SO), the 1015 to Pantyffynnon (6B09, SX) and the 2005 to Pantyffynnon (6B55, SX). Containerised coal for shipment to Northern Ireland leaves on either the 0510 to Swansea docks (6B51, MSX) or the 2045 service, bound for

Ellesmere Port (6M15, MSX Y).

There are also four daily diagrams for trainloads of coal in MDV wagons. These operate on a conditional basis and are bound for Swansea docks (two), Abercwmboi and Cardiff Tidal yard. Access to the washery at Coed Bach is via a new connection installed at Kidwelly in September 1983. Previously trains travelled to Burry Port along the BPGV line.

Left: CWMMAWR: Class 08 No. 08994 was rebuilt for the Cwmmawr branch in 1987. It is seen stabled at the open-cast disposal point on July 13 1988. Wagons for the afternoon trip to Coed Bach washery are being assembled on the left of the picture. The conversion of No. 08994 with a cut-down cab was undertaken to provide air-braked motive power for the Cwmmawr line. Detailed costings revealed that it was cheaper to convert the cab of an air-braked locomotive than to change the brakes on one of the three vacuum-braked Class 08s already cut-down. *MR.*

PANTYFFYNNON

THE *Railfreight* depot at Pantyffynnon exists to cater for coal movements from local mines. It also functions as a *Speedlink Coal* marshalling yard with daily *Speedlink Coal* services to: Radyr (6B07, FO Y, 0610); Coed Bach (6B02, SX, 0747; 6B54, SX, 1800); Newport Dock Street (6B07, MSX, 0755); Didcot (6A35, SX, 1745) and Washwood Heath (6M05, SX, 2325). Opencast coal is collected from Cwmmawr and Coed Bach (See page 61). Coal also arrives from Gwaun cae Gurwen, an opencast disposal point for the sites at East Pit and Garnant, both of which produce high quality anthracite. During 1988, output from 'GCG' has been poor but traffic was expected to flow again from September 1988.

Two deep mines serviced by Pantyffynnon are at Bettws (Ammanford) and Abernant. Abernant pit was opened in 1958 and produced 185,000 tons of anthracite in 1986. Coal output ceased at Abernant early in 1988 but rail traffic has actually increased along the Abernant line. BC reorganisation in 1988 led to the closure of Wernos washery at Pantyffynnon, where coal from Bettws drift mine had been washed. This coal is now washed at Abernant and this requires seven return trips each day along the branch. A single Class 37 hauls coal in a set of 18 HAAs. In this way the 375,000 ton annual output of Bettws drift mine can be washed and returned to Pantyffynnon yard for *Speedlink* distribution. Bettws is the newest pit in Wales, opened in 1978. It has also won a prestigious Business and Industry award for its environmental quality!

Below: PANTYFFYNNON: On April 2 1988, No. 37697 stands at the head of 6C16, the 1555 Pantyffynnon - Radyr *Speedlink Coal* duty. In 1988, this has been replaced by the tea-time service to Didcot. On this occasion, the train consisted of just three HEA hoppers; two for Exmouth Junction coal depot and one for Drinnick Mill. The large silo contains sand for locomotives about to climb to Abernant. *MR.*

Above: PANTYFFYNNON YARD:
On April 2 1987, Pantyfynon yard is filled with coal traffic. Cawoods containers (on the left) contain coal for Ireland. In the centre of the small yard are HEA hoppers loaded for *Speedlink Coal* distribution, whilst on the right is Class 37 No.37248, in charge of a 'trip' to Bettws drift mine. *MR.*

Left: GWAUN-CAE-GURWEN; The afternoon 'trip' from Gwaun-cae-Gurwen to Pantyffynnon pauses whilst the guard closes the crossing gates at 'GCG'. Class 37 No. 37241 is hauling FPA containers bound for Ellesmere Port and a rake of HEA hoppers for various domestic coal depots. In 1987, the train was coded as 6A78, 1450 'GCG' to Pantyffynnon, but in 1988 this became 6B13, 13.00 'GCG'- Pantyffynnon. This picture was taken on April 2 1987. *MR.*

Above: ABERNANT: On June 18 1982, when Abernant colliery was still producing coal, Class 37s Nos. 37251 & 37239 stand at the head of the afternoon trip to Pantyffynnon. Class 08 No. 08637 is lurching along the rickety sidings; it was on loan from BR at this time. Although Abernant produces no coal these days, its washery is used to process output from Bettws drift mine, as described in the text. *MR.*

Right: BETTWS DRIFT: Class 37 No. 37248 stands in the sidings at Bettws drift, on April 2 1987, with a trainload of coal for washing at Abernant. The train must run round in Pantyffynnon yard for this journey. *MR.*

WEST WALES

FREIGHT traffic beyond Kidwelly is sparse. A single daily *Speedlink* service visits all the *Speedlink* terminals in West Wales. The 0325 (SX) Gloucester-Trecwn (7B54) arrives at Trecwn at 1101. Here it services the government stores depot before returning to Gloucester via a stop at Haverfordwest (1343 -1443) and Camarthen (1543-1820). Eventual arrival back in Gloucester is at 2356. The service may be extended to Milford Haven if there is traffic from the government stores depot at Milford. A single weekly train of fertilizer runs from Ince and Elton to Carmarthen, the 1726 to Ince-Carmarthen (6V35).

Apart from the two diagrams already described, the only traffic west of Carmarthen is oil. The refineries at Robeston and Waterston generate 20 weekly trains to various oil depots and industrial consumers. The daily departures are outlined in the table on page 67.

Left: WATERSTON: The 1530 Waterston-West Bromwich Albion service (6M50) is seen leaving the refinery at Waterston on July 10 1984 behind Class 47 No. 47002. In 1988, the Albion service was rescheduled to run later, at 1842, and is coded 6M18. *PDS.*

Above: FERRYSIDE: The pleasing contour of the West Wales coast at Ferryside is the setting for this view of Class 47 No. 47350 at the head of 6M50, the 1530 Waterston-Albion tank train. *MR*

Right: FISHGUARD & GOODWICK: In 1982, the daily freight to the RNAD depot at Trecwn ran from Llandeilo Junction and serviced the coal depot at Fishguard. On August 27 1982, Class 37 No. 37266 arrives at Fishguard with a train of VVV vans containing government stores. In the background, Class 08 No. 08591 is the yard pilot at Goodwick. In 1988, Trecwn is served by a *Speedlink* service from Gloucester; the train now runs round at Letterston Junction and the coal depot at Fishguard has closed. *MR.*

Left: MILFORD HAVEN - Government stores are occasionally despatched by rail from Milford Haven. On August 27 1982, Class 47 No. 47129 leaves Milford with 7C45 to Llandeilo Junction. Traffic from Milford is dealt with by the Gloucester *Speedlink* in 1988. *MR.*

OIL TRAFFIC WEST OF CARMARTHEN, FROM AUGUST 1988.

CODE	FROM	TO	DEP	DAYS
6A08	Robeston	Langley	0050	TThSO
6A18	Robeston	Theale	0455	SX
6M18	Waterston	Albion	1842	SX
6M51	Waterston	Weaste	2040	TThO Y
6M51	Robeston	Cowley Hill	"	"
6M51	Robeston	Ravenhead Junction	"	"
6M27	Waterston	Albion	2210	MWFO
6C05	Waterston	Heathfield	2330	MO
6A14	Robeston	Theale	2327	FO

SHREWSBURY, WREXHAM & ABERYSTWYTH

Above: CRAVEN ARMS: Class 47 No. 47094 runs under clear lower quadrant signals at Craven Arms with the 0807 Ravenscraig-Severn Tunnel Junction steel 'empties' of August 9 1982. *PDS.*

SHREWSBURY is the meeting point of railway routes from Wolverhampton, Crewe, Wrexham, Aberystwyth and Hereford. The busiest route for freight traffic is the 'North and West' line, lying on the Hereford-Shrewsbury-Crewe axis, but the other routes also carry varying amounts of freight. Details of scheduled services passing through Shrewsbury are given in the accompanying table (See pages 69/70)

In Shrewsbury itself, Coton Hill yard remains open as a centre for local *Speedlink* traffic. It is connected to the main network by a daily working from Bescot, which also serves terminals at Oakengates, Wellington, Donnington and Alscott before returning to Bescot. This explains why Norsk Hydro fertiliser vans (used on Immingham-Alscott traffic) may be seen at Coton Hill. A Class 08 is available for local 'trip' workings in the Shrewsbury area, and in Summer 1988 this still included a visit to the oil terminal at

Shrewsbury Abbey, the site of the Shropshire & Montgomeryshire Railway's original terminus. The oil traffic originated at Bromford Bridge (Esso), but the last delivery was made on July 15 1988.

Concentration depots for domestic coal are located at Shrewsbury New Yard and Gobowen, both operated by J. Smallshaw. These are both served directly by a *Speedlink Coal* Network service from Washwood Heath, which on its outward journey runs out on the Crewe line to New Yard to detach loaded wagons and attach 'empties' before setting back into Shrewsbury station and taking the line to Gobowen. Haulage is generally by a Class 37/0 locomotive allocated to Cardiff Canton.

Gobowen is also the junction for the single-

SHREWSBURY: NORTHBOUND FREIGHT TRAFFIC FROM AUGUST 1988

CODE	TRAIN DETAILS	TIME AT SHREWSBURY ARR	DEP	TRAFFIC
7M58	2115 FSX Llanwern-Crewe	0024(pass)		Coal (ety)
6M45	2035 MWFO Barry Docks-Burn Naze	0041*	0300	Chemicals
6M18	1842 MWFO Waterston-Albion	0125 (pass) +		Oil
6M14	2050 SuO Abercwmboi-Ellesmere Port	0134(pass)		Cawoods Coal
6M45	1820 Waterston-Glazebrook	0155(pass)		Oil
6M14	2155 MO Abercwmboi-Ellesmere Port	0214(pass)		Cawoods Coal
6M15	2045 MSX Coedbach-Ellesmere Port or 2030 MSX Onllwyn-Ellesmere Port	0214(pass)		Cawoods Coal
6M51	2040 TThO Waterston-Weaste or 2040 TThO Robeston-Cowley Hill or Ravenhead	0309*	0311	Oil
6M78	2155 SX Bridgend-Warrington WOJ	0352(pass)		Speedlink
6M70	0010 MWFO Baglan Bay-Partington	0433*	0435	Chemicals
6M47	0250 SO Llanwern-Dee Marsh Jn.	0602*	0604	Steel
7J36	0503 SX Bescot-Coton Hill	0610(pass)		Speedlink
6M44	0145 MX Cardiff Tidal-Dee Marsh Jn.	0701*	0703	Steel
6M33	0710 SX Llanwern-Dee Marsh Jn.	1040*	1055	Steel
7J02	1000 SX Bescot-Blodwell	1109*	1111	Ballast (ety)
6J43	0920 SX Washwood Heath-Gobowen	1217(pass)$		Speedlink Coal
6S60	0900 SO Coedbach-Mossend	1431(pass)		Speedlink Coal
6J65	1315 MWFO Curzon Street-Penyffordd	1507(pass)		Cement (ety)
7F79	1524 WO Aberystwyth-Stanlow	1854(pass)		Oil (ety)
6S74	1645 SX Cardiff Tidal-Mossend	2059*	2114	Speedlink
4S81	1830 SX Pengam-Coatbridge	2213(pass)		Freightliner
6M46	2000 SX Cardiff Tidal-Warrington WOJ	2323(pass)		Speedlink
6M22	1305 MO Truro-Ince	2338(pass)		Fertiliser (ety)
6M22	1920 WO Carmarthen-Ince	2338(pass)		Fertiliser (ety)

* Calls for operating purposes only
+ Does not pass through Shrewsbury station. Time given at Sutton Bridge Jn.
$ See text for further details

Left: COTON HILL: On August 13 1987, Class 37 No. 37235 is pictured leaving Shrewsbury Coton Hill yard with 7G19, the 1339 *Speedlink* 'feeder' service to Bescot. The only traffic on this occasion is two empty oil tanks, returning from Shrewsbury Abbey (now closed) to Bromford Bridge. On the left is the former GWR main line to Wrexham and Chester. *PDS.*

CODE	TRAIN DETAILS	TIME AT SHREWSBURY		TRAFFIC
		ARR	DEP	
4V63	1805 SX Coatbridge-Pengam	0116(pass)		Freightliner
6V26	2120 SuO Burn Naze-Barry Docks	0137*	0146	Chemicals (ety)
6V26	2115 WFO Burn Naze-Barry Docks	0144*	0146	Chemicals (ety)
6J28	0116 WO Stanlow-Aberystwyth	0336(pass)		Oil
7V56	0254 MSX Crewe-Llanwern	0402(pass)		Coal
6V32	0500 TThSO Albion-Waterston	0638(pass) +		Oil (ety)
6V46	0440 MX Warrington Arpley-Cardiff Tidal	0647(pass)		Speedlink
6V07	0800 FSX Ellesmere Port-Coedbach or Onllwyn	1125(pass)		Cawoods coal (ety)
6V10	0800 FSO Ellesmere Port-Abercwmboi	1125(pass)		Cawoods coal (ety)
6V42	1128 SO Dee Marsh Jn. - Margam	1301*	1303	Steel (ety)
7G19	1315 SX Coton Hill -Bescot	1319(pass)		Speedlink
6V75	0635 SO Mossend-Cardiff Tidal	1348*	1350	Steel
6V65	1008 MO Glazebrook-Waterston	1348*	1350	Oil (ety)
6V65	1109 WFO Ravenhead-Robeston or 1104 WFO Cowley Hill-Robeston or 0954 WFO Weaste-Waterston	1348*	1350	Oil (ety)
6V39	0736 SO Mossend-Margam	1448*	1450	Steel
6V75	0635 MSX Mossend-Cardiff Tidal	1448*	1450	Steel
6G26	1557 SX Gobowen-Washwood Heath	1629(pass)		Speedlink Coal (ety)
7G25	1545 SX Blodwell-Bescot	1722*	1724	Ballast
6V39	0910 MSX Mossend-Cardiff Tidal	1745*	1747	Steel
6V35	1749 SuO Ince-Truro	1957(pass)		Fertiliser
6V71	1658 MWFO Partington-Baglan Bay	1958(pass)		Chemicals (ety)
6V35	1726 TO Ince-Carmarthen	1958(pass)		Fertiliser
6G65	2109 MWFO Penyffordd-Curzon Street	2226*	2234	Cement
6V86	2150 SX Warrington Arpley-Stoke Gifford	2355*	2357	Speedlink

*Calls for operating purposes only.   +Does not pass through Shrewsbury station. Time given at Sutton Bridge Jn.

track Blodwell branch, which is served by a daily ballast train from and to Bescot. Loading at Blodwell is scheduled for 1258-1545 (SX) and traction is usually provided by a Class 31 locomotive. This service is expected to cease in November 1988, after which the Blodwell branch is likely to close.

Petroleum from Stanlow is supplied in block trains to two receiving depots in the area under consideration. One destination is

Above: SHREWSBURY ABBEY: A delightful relic which survived well into the 1980s was the Esso oil terminal at Shrewsbury Abbey, served as required by a Class 08 'trip' from Coton Hill. On August 22 1985, No.08390 was chosen for this duty, and is seen here during shunting operations in the former Abbey station area. *PDS.*

Whittington, between Shrewsbury andGobowen. This is served by the 0537 (WFO) Stanlow-Whittington (6J26) and the 1612 (WFO return (7F28). The outward train runs first to either Haughton or Shrewsbury in order to run round and approach Whittington from the south.

The other destination is Aberystwyth, which is scheduled to receive a block train of 46-tonne tanks each Wednesday. This is now the only revenue-earning freight traffic over Cambrian lines. It is possible that the Aberystwyth oil train will be re-timed to

Above: SHREWSBURY (CREWE BANK): Class 37/7 No. 37894 passes Crewe Bank signal box, just north of Shrewsbury on the Crewe line, with an additional 0805 Abercwmboi-Ellesmere Port coal train (6Z41) on April 5 1988. The 27 PFAs are laden with Cawoods containers which will be shipped from Ellesmere Port to Ireland. _PDS._

operate during the night between Shrewsbury and Aberystwyth, after radio signalling becomes fully operational on this stretch.

Above: ABERYSTWYTH: After the demise of the Class 25s, twin Class 20 motive power became the norm for the Wednesdays-only Stanlow-Aberystwyth oil train. On April 6 1988, Nos. 20040 and 20170 were in charge, and are pictured here running round their train in Aberystwyth station. Part of the oil terminal is just visible beyond the platform on the left of the picture. PDS.

Right: BLODWELL: Class 25 No. 25042 draws its train of empty ballast hoppers under the loading apparatus at Blodwell on August 21 1985. The incoming service was 7J02, the 1012 Bescot-Blodwell duty, and the train would return loaded as 7G25, the 1528 Blodwell-Bescot. *PDS.*

Left: HAUGHTON:
Class 56 No.56088 nears
Haughton, on the
Shrewsbury-Gobowen
line, with a block load of
empty PCA cement
wagons from Birming-
ham Curzon Street to
Penyffordd, on the
evening of April 19
1985. *PDS.*

Above: LEATON: Since the advent of the *Speedlink Coal* network in 1986/7, Gobowen has become the destination of a daily train from Washwood Heath, bringing fuel to J. Smallshaw's depot at Shrewsbury Crewe Bank, as
well as to Gobowen. On August 13 1987, there was only one empty HEA to be recovered from Gobowen, so No.
37159 had an easy task with the return 6G26, 1830 Gobowen-Washwood Heath working, illustrated here. The
location is Leaton, four miles north of Shrewsbury. *PDS.*

DEESIDE

RAILFREIGHT'S fortunes on Deeside have improved greatly in recent years. A positive indication of this was the reinstatement of the direct link between Dee Marsh Junction and Mickle Trafford on September 1 1986. The line had been closed as an economy measure in May 1984 and traffic diverted via Wrexham, but an upturn in traffic justified its re-opening as a single-track route, with simplified signalling arrangements at each end. In 1988 the line carries three steel trains and one *Speedlink* service in each direction.

The most important freight customer on Deeside is British Steel. From 1952 until 1980, iron ore was carried from Bidston Dock to Shotwick Sidings, but this traffic ceased when steel-making came to an end at Shotton, whereupon many of the wagons were transferred to the Peak District for use on ICI limestone trains.

In 1988, the principal rail traffic at BSC Shotton is hot rolled coil, from steel-making plants at Ravenscraig, Llanwern and Port Talbot. The weekly traffic schedule at the time of writing (August 1988) is as follows:

ARRIVALS:

6M25: 0137 (daily) Mossend-Dee Marsh Junction. Arr. 0657.

6M47: 0250 (SO) Llanwern-Dee Marsh Junction. Arr. 0739.

6M44: 0145 (MX) Cardiff Tidal-Dee Marsh Junction. Arr. 0836.

6M24: 0525 (daily) Mossend-Dee Marsh Junction. Arr. 1056.

6M33: 0710 (SX) Llanwern-Dee Marsh Junction. Arr. 1306.

6M23: 1120 (SX) Mossend-Dee Marsh Junction. Arr. 1736

Below: WREXHAM: Approaching Wrexham on September 26 1987 is one of the dedicated South Wales Metals fleet, No. 37901 *Mirrlees Pioneer*, heading 6M44, the 0245 Severn Tunnel Junction-Dee Marsh Junction service. The 13 BBA/BAA wagons are carrying hot rolled steel coil from Llanwern to Shotton. *PDS.*

DEPARTURES:

6S42: 0820 (daily) Dee Marsh Junction - Mossend.

6V42: 1128 (SO) Dee Marsh Junction - Margam.

6S50: 1236 (daily) Dee Marsh Junction - Mossend.

6S47: 1920 (SX) Dee Marsh Junction - Mossend.

The Mossend trains carry coil from Ravenscraig and are hauled by pairs of Class 20 locomotives between Warrington Bank Quay and Dee Marsh Junction. The Llanwern and Cardiff trains each convey traffic from Port Talbot and/or Llanwern and are diagrammed for haulage by Class 37/9 locomotives from the South Wales Metals fleet. Readers will no doubt be puzzled by the imbalance of workings to and from South Wales. This is because most wagons carrying steel from South Wales to Shotton are sent

Above: SEALAND: On the re-opened Dee Marsh Junction-Mickle Trafford line, Class 20s Nos.20154 and 20009 approach the site of Sealand station with 6S50, the 1311 'empties' from Dee Marsh Junction to Mossend, on October 17 1987. The Class 20s will be exchanged for electric traction at Warrington Bank Quay. *PDS.*

empty from Shotton to Ravenscraig before returning with Scottish steel to South Wales. Thus, BR is able to achieve very good wagon utilisation with the minimum of 'empty' mileage.

Speedlink trains operate between Warrington and Deeside as follows:

7D26: 0625 (SX) Warrington Arpley-Shotton Paper Company, calling at Chester, Wrexham, Penyffordd and Dee Marsh Junction.

7F08: 1155 (SX) Shotton Paper Company-Warrington WOJ, calling at Dee Marsh Junction, Penyffordd, Wrexham and Chester.

6F51: 1935 (SX) Warrington Arpley-Dee Marsh Junction (via re-opened line).

Right: DEE MARSH : On August 15 1984, No. 56061 is pictured after arriving with a loaded steel coil train from Ravenscraig. On the left is a rake of POA scrap wagons, for Aldwarke. *David Allen.*

Below: ROSSETT: No. 25268 passes Rossett, between Wrexham and Chester, with the 1521 Dee Marsh Junction-Warrington *Speedlink* 'trip' (6F81) of April 19 1985. The formation is: 2 BBA (empty from BSC Shotton), 5 POA (scrap from BSC Shotton to Sheffield), 1 PCA (cement from Penyffordd). Rossett's semaphore signals were removed when this stretch of line was singled in early 1986. *PDS.*

6F69: 2129 (SX) Dee Marsh Junction - Warrington WOJ (via re-opened line).

The freight conveyed on these services includes a small amount of scrap metal from BSC Shotton to the Sheffield area, and traffic for two further customers of more recent origin. One is the Deeside Titanium Plant, constructed in 1980 on the site of Stewart & Lloyd's works, which receives occasional tank loads of chemicals from mainland Europe. The other is the Shotton Paper Company, established in the early 1980s near the site of Shotwick Sidings. The principal traffic to the Shotton Paper Company is raw timber, generally loaded on OTA wagons. Points of origin recorded in 1988 were Inverurie, Huntly, Keith, Elgin, Nairn, Fort William, Carmarthen, Exeter and Crawley.

There is also a small amount of outward paper traffic from Shotton to the Continent.

Further down the line towards Wrexham is the Castle Cement works at Penyffordd. A company train runs on Mondays, Wednesdays and Fridays from Penyffordd to Birmingham (Curzon Street), also conveying traffic for Oakengates. This is scheduled to arrive at Penyffordd at 1618, and depart again at 2109. There is *Speedlink* traffic from Penyffordd to Bangor, and also between Penyffordd and other Castle Cement works at Tring Cutting and Clitheroe. Wrexham itself is host to a steel terminal, operated by Williams, adjacent to BR's Watery Road freight terminal. Here, steel billets from ASW Brymbo are loaded for transfer by *Speedlink* to Cardiff Rod Mill.

THE NORTH WALES COAST

SINCE 1970 the freight scene at Holyhead has been dominated by the container terminal, situated adjacent to the passenger station on the east side of the harbour. There are daily *Freightliner* workings between Holyhead and Manchester (Trafford Park), Birmingham (Lawley Street) and London (Willesden / Stratford), with a fourth working to and from Crewe (Basford Hall) for connections with other trunk services. These are all booked for Class 47 haulage.

Also on the Isle of Anglesey is the Associated Octel chemicals plant at Amlwch, now the sole source of revenue on BR's 17-mile branch from Gaerwen. It was in honour of the Associated Octel traffic that Class 31 locomotive No.31296 was named *Tren Nwyddau Amlwch / Amlwch Freighter* in September 1986, an event which attracted much publicity in this normally quiet part of the world. In 1988, the staple freight service is provided by a daily block train from Ellesmere Port to Amlwch and back. For

Above: CONWY: *Railfreight*-liveried Class 31 No. 31275 has just crossed the Conwy estuary with 7P40, the twice-weekly nuclear flask train from Valley to Sellafield, on April 8 1988. Behind each flask carrier is an HEA coal hopper used as a barrier vehicle. *PDS.*

operating purposes, both workings are recessed for several hours at Llandudno Junction yard (see table), but no traffic is normally detached or attached there. The main commodities conveyed on this service are liquid chlorine from Ellesmere Port to Amlwch and ethylene dibromide from Amlwch to Ellesmere Port, together with lesser quantities of bromine from Amlwch, destined for mainland Europe. At the time of writing, Amlwch also receives raw sulphur from Mostyn Dock by rail, using an elderly fleet of HJV hopper wagons. These trains are not timetabled, and their operation depends on the arrival of ships at Mostyn. When they do run, their journey is usually broken at Llandudno Junction, as with the scheduled chemicals train mentioned already. It seems

Right: HOLYHEAD CONTAIN-ER TERMINAL: Class 47 No. 47106 leaves the Container Terminal at Holyhead with 4K59, the 1705 *Freightliner* service to Crewe Basford Hall, on April 17 1985. At Crewe the train will connect with trunk *Freightliner* services. *PDS.*

NORTH WALES COAST: PRINCIPAL FREIGHT SERVICES FROM AUGUST 1988

DOWN

CODE	TRAIN DETAILS	TIME AT LLANDUDNO JCT ARR	DEP	DAYS	TRAFFIC
7D56	0100 Ellesmere Port - Llandudno Jn.	0251		MX	Chemicals
6M43	2201 (TO) Humber O.R. - Holyhead	0402*	0409	WO	Petroleum Coke
7D04	0550 Llandudno Jn. - Amlwch		0550	SX	Chemicals
7D14	0443 Warrington Arpley - Llandudno Jn.	0626		MX	Speedlink
7D30	0557 Crewe - Penmaenmawr	0746*	0748	SX	Ballast (ety)
4D52	0712 Crewe - Holyhead	0904(pass)		MX	Freightliner
6D02	0547 Carnforth - Penmaenmawr	0926*	1011	SX	Ballast (ety)
6D25	0812 Fiddlers Ferry - Point of Ayr			MSX	MGR (ety)
6D03	0835 Bamber Bridge or 0806 Carnforth - Penmaenmawr	1209*	1236	SX	Ballast (ety)
6D25	1012 Fiddlers Ferry - Point of Ayr			MO	MGR (ety)
6D04	1020 Washwood Heath - Penmaenmawr	1433*	1511	FO	Stone (ety)
6D04	1128 Ashburys - Penmaenmawr	1543*	1553	FSX	Stone (ety)
4D59	1554 Trafford Park - Holyhead	1832(pass)		SX	Freightliner
4D58	1515 Lawley Street - Holyhead	1905 (pass)		SX	Freightliner
4D62	1625 Willesden - Holyhead	2126(pass)		SX	Freightliner

UP

CODE	TRAIN DETAILS	TIME AT LLANDUDNO JCT ARR	DEP	DAYS	TRAFFIC
4G66	0410 Holyhead - Lawley Street	0503(pass)		SO	Freightliner
7F62	0515 Point of Ayr - Fiddlers Ferry			MSX	MGR
4G66	0542 Holyhead - Lawley Street	0630 (pass)		MSX	Freightliner
7F62	0655 Point of Ayr - Fiddlers Ferry			MO	MGR
4H59	0622 Holyhead - Trafford Park	0718*	0724	SX	Freightliner
4L86	0643 Holyhead - Stratford	0745 (pass)		MSX	Freightliner
6E36	0742 Holyhead - Humber OR	0843*	0921	ThO	Petr. coke (ety)
7K11	1011 Penmaenmawr - Crewe	1021*	1023	SX	Ballast
7D05	0900 Amlwch - Llandudno Jn.	1036		SX	Chemicals
6P14	1239 Penmaenmawr - Carnforth	1239*	1251	SX	Ballast
6F16	1420 Llandudno Jn. - Warrington W.O.J.		1420	SX	Speedlink
6P15	1513 Penmaenmawr - Carnforth/Bamber Bridge	1523*	1525	SX	Ballast
4K59	1756 Holyhead - Crewe	1850(pass)		SX	Freightliner
6H19	1917 Penmaenmawr - Ashburys	1927*	1929	FSX	Stone
6J19	1917 Penmaenmawr - Salford Hope Street	1927*	1929	FO	Stone
7F18	2058 Llandudno Jn. - Ellesmere Port		2058	SX	Chemicals
4L86	2305 Holyhead - Stratford	2359(pass)		SuO	Freightliner

* Calls for operating purposes only.

Right: HOLYHEAD DIESEL DEPOT: *Railfreight* -liveried No. 47285 joins the main line on April 8 1988, with the daily Target 92 'trip' working to Llandudno Junction. The train includes an empty TTA from Holyhead fuelling point (to Stanlow), two HEA hoppers and a CAR brake van. The HEAs had been used as barrier wagons for nuclear flask traffic and, along with the brake van, had been collected earlier from Valley CEGB sidings. On the right is Holyhead fuelling point and on the left are the private sidings of Stockton Haulage. *PDS.*

likely that the Mostyn-Amlwch flow will cease in late 1988 or early 1989, possibly to be replaced by a new flow of liquid sulphur from Runcorn (Folly Lane).

Penmaenmawr quarries have been producing railway ballast for over a century, and traffic levels remain high in 1988, with three scheduled departures each weekday. Revenue-earning traffic from Penmaenmawr was until recently limited to a weekly vacuum-braked train to Salford (Hope Street). In March 1987, however, a new arrangement came into operation, whereby the Hope Street flow is covered by resources from the Peak Forest - Washwood Heath circuit; two Class 37 locomotives and a rake of RMC-liveried PHA hoppers. Initially a Penmaenmawr - Hope

Left: HOLYHEAD ANGLESEY ALUMINI- UM: 'Target 92' is illustrated once more on April 8 1988, this time just after calling at the Anglesey Aluminium plant to collect a high capacity ferry van (loaded with aluminium ingots) which is now marshalled next to the locomotive. This ferry van and the empty oil tank will continue their journey from Llandudno Junction on 6F16, the 1445 *Speedlink* 'feeder' service to Warrington. *PDS.*

Right: LLANFAIR PG: No. 47647 passes the re-opened Llanfair PG station on April 7 1988 with the Thursdays-only petroleum coke 'empties' from Holyhead (Anglesey Aluminium) to Immingham (Humber Oil Refinery). The train is designated 6E36, the 0740 Holyhead-Immingham. *PDS.*

Above: GAERWEN: On the damp and drizzly afternoon of August 11 1987, No. 47334 sets back on to the Up line at Gaerwen with 15 HJVs loaded with sulphur from Mostyn Dock to Amlwch. Note the use of a traditional short-wheelbase van (ex-VVV) next to the locomotive, its main purpose being to carry wagon sheets when the train returns empty to Mostyn. The train had been stabled at Llandudno Junction overnight, and this section of the working was designated 8L40, 1100 Llandudno Junction-Amlwch. Here at Gaerwen the train has had to cross over on to the Up line in order to gain access to the Amlwch branch. *PDS.*

Street working ran in place of the Washwood Heath train each Friday, but traffic levels to Washwood Heath have been increased, and since July 1988 the train is scheduled to serve Washwood Heath as normal on Friday morning and then proceed empty to Penmaenmawr, loaded to Hope Street, and back to Peak Forest. Another new flow to start during 1987 is stone from Penmaenmawr to Ashburys, routed via Crewe in both directions. These trains run four times a week with Class 47 motive power and POA wagons.

Three further company trains run along the North Wales Coast line. One brings petroleum coke once a week from

Left: AMLWCH: No. 47128 leaves the Associated Octel terminal at Amlwch with 7D05, the 0825 to Llandudno Junction, on April 18 1985. The train consists of four loaded ethylene dibromide tanks and four empty chlorine tanks, plus the obligatory brake van and barrier vehicle at each end of the formation. *PDS.*

Immingham (Humber Refinery) to Holyhead (Anglesey Aluminium), using a dedicated fleet of covered hopper wagons. The second operation conveys nuclear flask traffic for Wylfa and Trawsfynydd power stations: a twice-weekly trunk train runs from Sellafield to Valley, where a road connection is made to and from Wylfa, whilst Trawsfynydd traffic is detached at Llandudno Junction

and taken along the Conwy Valley in a separate 'trip' working. Thirdly, at the eastern end of the Coast line, coal is forwarded from the last rail-connected pit in North Wales, at Point of Ayr. This usually takes the form of a daily train to Fiddlers Ferry, hauled by a pair of Class 20 locomotives, but other destinations may be served from time to time, such as Oakleigh (ICI) and Ironbridge.

All *Speedlink* traffic to and from the North Wales Coast is conveyed by a daily working from Warrington to Llandudno Junction and back. Some of the traffic is for Llandudno Junction itself, whilst distribution to other terminals in North Wales is effected by two 'trip' workings. One, known as 'Target 92',

Below: BANGOR STATION: A bird's eye view of Bangor station on the evening of August 10 1987, showing 47476 on the Down 'through' line with the 1554 Trafford Park-Holyhead *Freightliner* and a Class 150/2 *Sprinter* unit in the Up loop with the 1950 departure to Leeds. The former locomotive depot is visible on the right hand side of the picture, and the goods yard is further still to the right. *PDS.*

Top: PENMAENMAWR: Pictured during loading at Penmaenmawr on April 7 1988 is *Railfreight*-liveried Class 47 No. 47318, with a rake of 29 POA open wagons. These will form 6L82, the 1855 'special' working to Ashburys, a train which has since been incorporated into the timetable as 6H19. On the right are some of the extensive earthworks for the A55 North Wales Expressway. *PDS*.

Above: CONWY MORFA: Whilst the new A55 may pose a threat to BR's North Wales Coast Line in the long term, the project is at least bringing substantial freight traffic to the railway during the construction period. This photograph shows the purpose-built terminal at Conwy Morfa on the morning of April 8 1988, with No.47366 propelling BDA steel carriers into the sidings. The steel had come from Cardiff. *PDS*.

serves Bangor and Holyhead, generally leaving Llandudno Junction in the early morning and returning around lunchtime. Traction is usually provided by the Class 47 from 7D14. The other 'trip' working, 'Target 90', is an afternoon train from Llandudno Junction to Maentwrog Road siding, running only when required. A fair variety of merchandise is carried by *Speedlink* in North Wales. The freight depot at Llandudno Junction, opened in 1981 to replace facilities lost elsewhere in the A55 construction works, receives fuel oil from Stanlow (BP), domestic coal from South Wales and the Midlands, and (since Summer 1988) incoming timber from Chichester. Steel for the A55 is handled both at Llandudno Junction and at the purpose-built terminal at Conwy Morfa, whilst Conwy Morfa is also the destination for cement from Penyffordd and trainloads of sand from Widnes. Maentwrog Road is the rail forwarding point for explosives traffic from Penrhyndeudraeth, although it is

understood that this will cease shortly. Bangor goods yard acts as a receiving depot for Blue Circle cement from Hope, and there is also Castle cement traffic from Penyffordd and Clitheroe. The Anglesey Aluminium plant has been mentioned above as receiving block loads of petroleum coke; *Speedlink* traffic includes aluminium billets for mainland Europe and small quantities of inwards chemicals. Holyhead itself is host to a Stockton Haulage terminal, handling general merchandise for Ireland, albeit on a much reduced scale compared with the Stranraer operation. Fuel oil is conveyed by *Speedlink* to Holyhead locomotive servicing depot.

Below: LLANDUDNO JUNCTION: On April 7 1988, *Speedlink Distribution*-liveried No. 47231 waits in Llandudno Junction yard with 6F16, the 1445 *Speedlink* working to Warrington. The formation comprises: five empty oil tanks from Llandudno Junction to Stanlow, one petroleum coke hopper (from the Immingham-Holyhead circuit) for repairs, two VDA vans, one empty BDA from Conwy Morfa, and one empty PCA returning from Bangor to Penyffordd. *PDS.*

Left: BLAENAU FFESTINIOG: Class 47 No. 47352 enters the 'new' station at Blaenau Ffestiniog on April 7 1988 with Target 90, conveying a VAA van loaded with explosives, en route from from Maentwrog Road to Snodgrass. On the right are the tracks of the Ffestiniog Railway, which was extended here in 1982, shortly after the opening of the BR station. *PDS.*

Below: MAENTWROG ROAD: The delightfully maintained privately-owned station building at Maentwrog Road sets the scene for this view of Class 25 No.25058, heading north with a nuclear flask from Trawsfynydd to Sellafield, on April 17 1985. *PDS.*

Right: SANDYCROFT - One of the short-lived Class 25/9 sub-class, No.25912, approaches Sandycroft on August 14 1986 with 7F18, the 1720 Llandudno Junction-Ellesmere Port chemicals train. This working is a continuation of 7D05 from Amlwch (see also page 81), and was re-timed in May 1987 to run during the hours of darkness. *PDS.*

SECTION 2: SCOTLAND

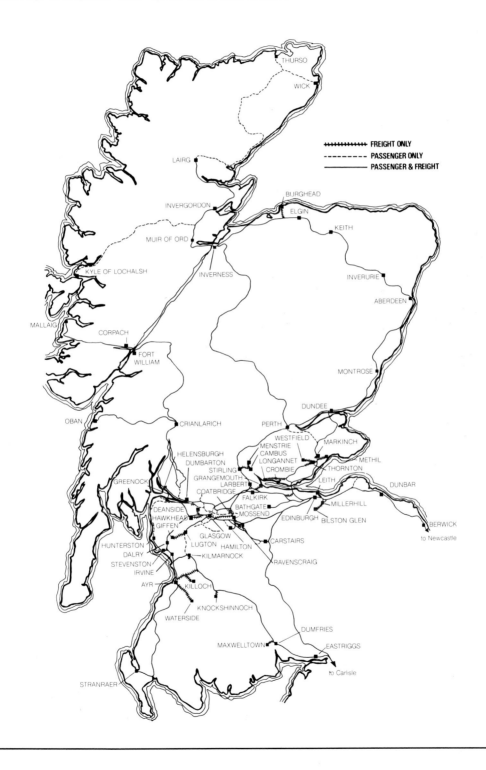

FREIGHT ONLY
PASSENGER ONLY
PASSENGER & FREIGHT

THURSO
WICK
LAIRG
INVERGORDON
BURGHEAD
ELGIN
KEITH
MUIR OF ORD
INVERNESS
KYLE OF LOCHALSH
INVERURIE
ABERDEEN
MALLAIG
CORPACH
FORT WILLIAM
MONTROSE
OBAN
CRIANLARICH
DUNDEE
PERTH
WESTFIELD
MARKINCH
HELENSBURGH
MENSTRIE
DUMBARTON
CAMBUS
METHIL
STIRLING
LONGANNET
THORNTON
GREENOCK
GRANGEMOUTH
CROMBIE
LARBERT
LEITH
COATBRIDGE
DUNBAR
FALKIRK
DEANSIDE
BATHGATE
MILLERHILL
HAWKHEAD
MOSSEND
GIFFEN
EDINBURGH
BILSTON GLEN
BERWICK
to Newcastle
GLASGOW
HUNTERSTON
LUGTON
CARSTAIRS
DALRY
HAMILTON
STEVENSTON
KILMARNOCK
IRVINE
RAVENSCRAIG
AYR
KILLOCH
KNOCKSHINNOCH
DUMFRIES
WATERSIDE
MAXWELLTOWN
EASTRIGGS
to Carlisle
STRANRAER

SOUTH WEST SCOTLAND

COAL is the most important source of freight traffic in South West Scotland. The main flow is from Knockshinnoch opencast site (near New Cumnock) to Ayr Harbour, where the coal is shipped to Northern Ireland for consumption at Belfast West power station. Knockshinnoch had been derelict since the closure of the deep mine shaft there in the late 1960s, but an EEC grant provided the basis for re-developing the site as an opencast disposal point, and by mid-1985 (after the end of the long miners' strike) coal trains were running once again from Knockshinnoch. Initially, the coal was carried in vacuum-braked HTV wagons, but these proved to be less than ideal, and in September 1985, Westinghouse door-closing equipment was installed at Ayr Harbour, to enable the use of air-braked 'merry-go-round' wagons (HAA) instead. At the time of writing there is a daily schedule of three trains each way between Knockshinnoch and Ayr, each comprising 32 HAAs hauled by a pair of Class 20 locomotives. At the Harbour a Class 08 pilot is employed to shunt the wagons in and out of the discharge terminal. In addition to the flow to Ayr Harbour, there is a fourth train from Knockshinnoch which runs on alternate weekdays, i.e. five times a fortnight, bringing coal for consumption at the Roche Products factory near Dalry. This is worked as a block train of 24 wagons as far as Falkland yard, and then the traffic is conveyed on specified *Speedlink* services, 12 wagons at a time between Falkland and Dalry.

Tied up with the success of *Railfreight's* new venture at Knockshinnoch was the re-opening of the line between Annbank and Mauchline on March 21 1988. This line had previously been closed under the Ayrshire

Below: STRANRAER HARBOUR: The Stranraer pilot locomotive, Class 08 No. 08737, shunts an empty PLA car-carrying wagon in the Harbour station area on July 25 1985, before working back to Stranraer Town sidings. The PLA will be included in the afternoon *Speedlink* service to Carlisle, which at that time was 6E85, the 1716 departure to Scunthorpe. *PDS.*

Above: KNOCKSHINNOCH: Class 20s Nos. 20192 and 20227 draw forward under the rapid loader at Knockshinnoch opencast disposal point on July 13 1988, after working the 0948 'empties' from Ayr Harbour. The train will return loaded as 6R04, the 1147 Knockshinnoch-Ayr Harbour. *PDS.*

Resignalling Scheme in 1985, necessitating a lengthy diversion via Barassie and Kilmarnock. Re-opening of the Mauchline to Annbank stretch was justified in 1988 because of the more efficient use of resources (especially locomotives) that could be made by sending the coal trains over the shorter route. The £200,000 re-opening costs were met by BR's Coal sub-sector alone. At the time of writing, all *Speedlink* and other freight services between Ayr and Carlisle are still routed via Kilmarnock, mainly to avoid possible pathing conflict with the coal trains, though it is possible that at least one non-coal train may be transferred to the re-opened link in early 1989. The resurgence of coal traffic in South West Scotland is not

limited to the Knockshinnoch - Ayr flow. Two more line re-openings are scheduled for late 1988/early 1989. First, the Waterside branch to the south of Ayr has been revived, together with a 1 1/2-miles extension from Waterside to a new British Coal opencast site at Chalmerston. The branch had been disused since the conventional colliery terminal at Waterside closed in Spring 1986. Trains began running on the branch again in October 1988, initially destined for Bilston Glen colliery for blending. The main flow from Chalmerston, however, will be shipment coal for Ayr harbour, starting in March 1989. This ties in with the final line reopening in SW Scotland, the Killoch branch. Killoch is the point at which coal from the Barony complex is brought to to the surface, and it also houses a washery for coal mined elsewhere. The only rail traffic from Killoch since the miners' strike has been very occasional block loads of slurry to Methil power station, loaded in MDV wagons. Starting in March 1989, however, the coal from

Above: BYREHILL JUNCTION : Passing the open but forlorn-looking signal box at Byrehill Junction on July 24 1985, is Class 25 No. 25201, heading the weekly nuclear flask train from Fairlie. The train has just traversed the 'freight only' curve from Dubbs Junction. Byrehill Junction signal box was closed under the 1985 Ayrshire Resignalling Scheme. *PDS.*

Above: AYR HARBOUR: The Ayr Harbour pilot locomotive, No. 08735, pulls a rake of HAAs out of the discharge terminal on the afternoon of July 15 1988. These will be stabled in the sidings on the left and will be included in the next train of 'empties' to Knockshinnoch, unless any need to be sent to Millerhill for repairs. *PDS.*

Chalmerston will be taken via Falkland yard to Killoch for washing, before being railed back to Ayr Harbour for export. Because of severe gradients on the Killoch branch, the 36-wagon trains operating out of Chalmerston will have to be re-marshalled into rakes of 24 wagons for the journey to Killoch.

Perhaps the most remarkable feature of the developments mentioned thus far is that they will, if all goes according to plan, all be accomplished without the need for extra locomotives. The pair of Class 20s currently plying between Knockshinnoch and Ayr on weekday mornings and afternoons will work to Chalmerston and Killoch both during the night and on Saturday mornings, and also to Killoch on alternate weekday afternoons, whenever the fourth Knockshinnoch train (for Dalry) does not run.

One further development in the movement of coal needs to be mentioned here, although

Left: HUNTERSTON: Class 37 locomotives Nos. 37137 and 37292 await departure from Hunterston High Level sidings with 6D14, the 1544 iron ore train to Ravenscraig, on July 24 1985. The line curving round to the left, beyond the fence, continues to Largs and has since been singled and electrified as part of the Ayrshire modernisation scheme. *PDS.*

AYR (FALKLAND JUNCTION YARD) TRUNK FREIGHT SERVICES FROM AUGUST 1988 *(See also text, p91)*

CODE	FROM	TO	TIME AT FALKLAND DEP	ARR	TRAFFIC	DAYS
6S66	Tyne	Stranraer	0315	0340	Speedlink	MX
6S45	Carlisle	Stranraer	0739	0813	Speedlink	MX
6R42	Grangemouth	Prestwick	0806	0852	Oil	MSX Y
6S59	Tees	Falkland	0954		Speedlink	MSX
6S59	Tees	Falkland	1058		Speedlink	SO
6E96	Stranraer	Tyne	1330	1500	Speedlink	SX
6D20	Falkland	Mossend		1655	Speedlink	SX
6E84	Stranraer	Scunthorpe	1813	1920	Speedlink	SX
6E95	Falkland	Tees		2122	Speedlink	SX

it is not wholly contained within Ayrshire. This is the new flow from Ravenstruther (near Carstairs) to Ayr Harbour, conveying coal from opencast sites in the Douglas Basin, due to start in January 1989, with a pair of locomotives hauling two 32-wagon trains there and back each weekday. With the new traffic from Chalmerston and Ravenstruther supplementing the established flow from Knockshinnoch, BR confidently expects the tonnage of coal through Ayr Harbour to double from its present figure of half a million tonnes to around one million tonnes per annum by the end of the decade. And now that the new Kilroot 2 Power Station has been confirmed to be a coal (not Irish lignite) burner, it is possible that even

this figure will be exceeded. In order to cater more effectively for such an increase, the track and hopper layout at Ayr Harbour has been re-built, with a financial contribution from the EEC and Associated British Ports.

Most *Speedlink* operations in South West Scotland are centred on Falkland yard, just to the north of Newton-on-Ayr station. The yard was modernised in 1985, and the sorting of *Speedlink* wagons is now concentrated on four long loops and twelve dead-end sidings on the up side of the line. Falkland is served by three trunk *Speedlink* workings each day from England (see table), two of which are extended to Stranraer, and one 'feeder' from ScotRail's principal yard at Mossend. The same pattern applies to outgoing *Speedlink* services from Falkland. Two local 'trip' workings operate each weekday from Falkland to individual freight terminals in the surrounding area. These are coded R02 and R05, and are diagrammed for Class 26 and Class 37 haulage respectively. 'Trip' R 02 operates between the hours of 0620 and 1630, and may serve Dalry (Roche), Stevenston Misk (ICI), Irvine (Blue Circle and Caberboard), Kilwinning lime siding, Glengarnock (Youngs) and Snodgrass (ICI) as required. 'Trip' R05 operates between 1100 and 1835 and may serve Kilmarnock Hill Street and Barleith (both Johnny Walker), Stevenston (ICI), Snodgrass (ICI), Kilwinning lime siding and Dalry (Roche). Commodities carried on the two 'trips' include chemicals, salt and coal to Dalry, a small amount of general merchandise traffic to and from

Glengarnock, chemicals to Stevenston, cement to Irvine (Blue Circle), resin and timber to Irvine (Caberboard), and agricultural lime to Kilwinning. The only regular outward traffic is bottled whisky from Kilmarnock and Barleith, destined for mainland Europe via the Dover-Dunkerque ferry.

Virtually all Stranraer's freight traffic is bound for Northern Ireland, by means of the Stranraer-Larne ferry. It can be divided into two groups. Firstly, motor vehicles from both British and foreign sources are conveyed to Stranraer Harbour, where they are unloaded by Sealink. Secondly, a wide range of commodities is handled by Stockton Haulage at their Stranraer Town terminal, for a short road transfer to the Harbour. The Stockton Haulage terminal was established with the aid of Scotland's first Section 8 Grant in

AYR (FALKLAND JUNCTION YARD) TRIP FREIGHT SERVICES, FROM AUGUST 1988					
CODE	LOCO	FROM (TIME)	TO (TIME)	TRAFFIC	DAYS
R02	26	Falkland (0620)	Dalry (0655)	Speedlink	SX
		Dalry (0717)	Stevenston (0728)	Speedlink	SX
		Stevenston (0748)	Falkland (0809)	LE	SX
		Falkland (0834)	Irvine (0916)	Speedlink	SX
		Irvine (0916)	Dalry (0947)	Speedlink	SX
		Dalry (0958)	Glengarnock (1030)	Speedlink	SX
		Glengarnock (1025)	Falkland (1058)	Speedlink	SX
		Falkland (1130)	Snodgrass (1215)	Speedlink	SX
		Snodgrass (1247)	Irvine (1252)	Speedlink	SX
		Irvine (1320)	Falkland (1340)	Speedlink	SX
		Works 6D20			
R04	2x20	Ayr harbour (0605)	Knockshinnoch (0712)	MGR	SX
		Knockshinnoch (0804)	Ayr harbour (0910)	MGR	SX
		Ayr harbour (0948)	Knockshinnoch (1055)	MGR	SX
		Knockshinnoch (1147)	Ayr harbour (1255)	MGR	SX
		Ayr harbour (1345)	Knockshinnoch (l453)	MGR	SX
		Knockshinnoch (1544)	Ayr harbour (1705)	MGR	SX
		Ayr harbour (1750)	Knockshinnoch (1914)	MGR	SX
		Knockshinnoch (2066)	Ayr harbour (2114)	MGR	SX
R05	37	Falkland (1100)	Kilmarnock (1130)	Speedlink	SX
		Kilmarnock (1217)	Falkland (1242)	Speedlink	SX
		Falkland (1405)	Stevenston (1435)	Speedlink	SX
		Stevenston (1517)	Snodgrass (1527)	Speedlink	SX
		Snodgrass (1602)	Falkland (1622)	Speedlink	SX
		Falkland (1635)	Dalry (1755)	LE	SX
		Dalry (1803)	Falkland (1835)	Speedlink	SX
R18	08	Falkland Junction yard pilot		Speedlink	SX
R19	08	Ayr harbour pilot		MGR	SX
R31	08	Stranraer pilot		Speedlink	Sun
R32	08	Stranraer pilot		Speedlink	SuX

The following diagrams exist for departmental traffic:-			
R07	26	Falkland (0850) ACE instructions, priority Hillhouse	SX
R08	26	Falkland (0600) ACE instructions, priority Hillhouse	SX
R10	08	Irvine PW depot/S & T workshops pilot	SX
R12	26	Falkland (2248) ACE instructions, priority Irvine ballast	SX
R14	26	Ayr TMD (0735), (1500), (2235). ACE instructions	SX
R15	26	Ayr TMD (2300) ACE instructions	SO
R16	26	Ayr TMD (2345) ACE instructions	SO
R17	any	Ayr TMD (0001) ACE instructions	SuO
R33	47	Stranraer Town (0545) ACE instructions	TWThO
		Loco works 6E96	

Below: DUMFRIES: Class 08 No. 08396 is about to set off down the Maxwelltown branch, at Dumfries, with a trainload of petroleum tanks for the South East Oils depot, on August 24 1981. In 1988 there is no longer a Class 08 stationed at Dumfries, and this branch is worked by the locomotive from the Carlisle-Dumfries 'trip', usually a Class 26. *PDS.*

1979, with the principal aim of handling heavy steel traffic from Teesside. Today, the steel traffic is as buoyant as ever, not only from Teesside but also from Scunthorpe, Etruria and other British Steel plants, and it has been supplemented by other goods such as cider from Taunton, resin from Duxford, chemicals from Wilton and fertiliser from Immingham. In addition to the export traffic handled at Stranraer, there is a seasonal flow of agricultural lime from Shap (Cumbria) to Stranraer Town for distribution locally by road.

Operations on the Stranraer line are somewhat hampered by the long 1 in 51 climb southwards from Girvan. This places severe limitations on the capacity of *Speedlink* services south of Falkland, to the extent that Stranraer-bound trains frequently have to be reduced in length before continuing their journey from Falkland. The following details illustrate the point:

MAXIMUM WEIGHT (INCL LOCOMOTIVE) IN CLASS 6 TIMINGS:

	Carlisle-Falkland	Falkland-Carlisle
Class 37:	950	500
Class 47:	1,327	632

MAXIMUM WEIGHT (INCL LOCOMOTIVE) IN CLASS 7 TIMINGS:

Class 37:	1,060	560
Class 47:	1,430	680

Sometimes, because of this restriction, there is too much traffic at Falkland to be conveyed on the two scheduled services to

Right: STRANRAER TOWN: The small but busy Stockton Haulage terminal at Stranraer Town is illustrated on July 25 1985, with Class 47 No. 47211 and a loaded BDA steel carrier in view. No. 47211 had just deposited the BDA after arriving with the 0509 *Speedlink* service from Carlisle. *PDS.*

Right: FALKLAND (NORTH END): The 1655 Falkland-Mossend *Speedlink* service is pictured departing from Falkland yard on July 11 1988, headed by Class 26 No. 26010. The formation comprises one empty OTA timber wagon from Irvine to the West Highland Line, and four HAA hoppers (from the Knockshinnoch-Ayr circuit) on their way to Millerhill wagon repair depot. On the far right, Class 20s Nos. 20192 and 20227 have just arrived with a coal train from Knockshinnoch. *PDS.*

Above: STEVENSTON: Class 37s Nos. 37320 and 37049 pass through Stevenston with an additional 6Z76 Hunterston-Ravenscraig ore train, on July 15 1988. No. 37049 is carrying the latest *Railfreight Coal* sub-sector livery. The siding on the left provides access to the ICI Misk terminal, located behind the photographer. *PDS.*

Stranraer. In these circumstances a third train may be provided by extending 6S59 (see table) from Falkland to Stranraer, departing at about 1030. A fresh locomotive will then have to be found for Falkland 'trip' R05, since 6S59 and R05 are officially covered by the same diagram.

Speedlink traffic to and from the Dumfries area is conveyed by two daily 'out and back'

workings from Carlisle yard. One serves the Ministry of Defence depot at Eastriggs, and the other serves Powfoot and Dumfries, with an extension when required to Maxwelltown. The only regular traffic at Dumfries itself is raw timber to Shotton. There are two terminals on the Maxwelltown branch: one is operated by South East Oils to receive petroleum traffic from Grangemouth refinery, and

Below: FALKLAND UP SIDINGS: No. 37066 waits in the Up yard at Falkland with 6S59, the 0135 Tees-Falkland *Speedlink* service of July 12 1988. The train had just arrived with four TTAs, carrying resin from Duxford to Irvine, plus several BDWs and BDAs, with steel from Lackenby to Stranraer. Because there was already a backlog of Stranraer-bound traffic at Falkland (see text) 6S59 was re-formed here and extended to Stranraer. All the wagons which had arrived on 6S59, with the exception of one BDW, were detached for onward movement by other services, and nine wagons which had been left at Falkland by 6S45 were then attached in order to bring the train up to the maximum permitted load. The formation on departure from Falkland was: 1 BDW (steel from Lackenby), 2 PJA (cars from Longbridge), 2 PQA (cars from Morris Cowley), 2 PQA (cars from Immingham), and 3 BDA (steel from Scunthorpe). *PDS*.

Left: EASTRIGGS: Class 40 No. 40155 shunts three air-braked vans into the sidings at Eastriggs, between Carlisle and Dumfries, after working the 6S87 'trip' freight from Carlisle yard, on July 16 1984. Access to the sidings is controlled by the ground frame in the centre of the picture. Eastriggs remains an active location in 1988, but 40155 was withdrawn from service in January 1985. *PDS*.

the other is used by ICI for both inward and outward chemicals traffic.

Block petroleum trains run from Grangemouth to two terminals in South West Scotland. Aviation fuel is delivered in 102-tonne and 46-tonne tanks to Prestwick, and fuel oil is conveyed in 46-tonne tanks to Riccarton, just outside Kilmarnock. The Riccarton train is scheduled to run every Monday, with the loaded train leaving Grangemouth at 0531 and the return 'empties' departing at 1515. Both workings are routed via Paisley and Barassie (reverse), in order to avoid possible congestion on the single line between Barrhead and Kilmarnock. The service to Prestwick is less predictable. One train runs daily (MSX to either Prestwick or Paisley Hawkhead (see page 98) according to demand, with Prestwick being served twice in an 'average' week. All the petroleum trains are booked for Class 37 haulage.

The Largs branch is kept busy with trainloads of imported coal and iron ore from Hunterston (High Level) to British Steel Ravenscraig. This traffic recovered well after the miners' strike and is now operating more intensively than ever. The coal trains consist of 46 HAAs, and the iron ore trains comprise 21 PTAs. Departure times from Hunterston (correct to August 1988) are: 0155 MX (ore), 0318 MX (coal), 0526 SO (coal), 0820 EWD (ore), 1025 EWD (coal), 1103 EWD (ore), 1430 SX (coal), 1610 SX (ore), 1827 SX (ore), 2035 SX (ore), and 2326 SX (coal). Both types of train are hauled by paired Class 37 locomotives based at Motherwell. In 1986 a dedicated fleet was set up to operate the five Hunterston - Ravenscraig diagrams and renumbered into the 373xx series. This fleet had been partly disbanded by Summer 1988 but BR was intending to allocate a fresh set of locomotives to the work as this book went to press. In the longer term, it is hoped that some of the first Class 60 freight locomotives may be used on the Hunterston trains, releasing the Class 37s to replace ScotRail's life-expired Class 20s in turn.

Several miscellaneous freight flows in South West Scotland remain to be mentioned. Ayr Harbour, in addition to its major role as a coal export terminal, is used as a railhead for exported cement traffic from Uddingston, and from 1987 until 1989 there is also steel traffic from Scunthorpe to Ayr Harbour, ultimately destined for Faslane on the north bank of the Clyde. From Fairlie, on the Largs branch, a weekly nuclear flask train runs to the Sellafield re-processing plant in Cumbria. Finally, the new Caledonian Paper

Above: KILMARNOCK: Johnny Walker's terminal at Kilmarnock Hill Street, July 12 1988, with Falkland 'trip' R05 in attendance. Three of the loaded ferry vans went to Falkland yard for attachment to the next Carlisle *Speedlink*. No. 26037 was a replacement for the rostered Class 37, which had worked to Stranraer with an extended 6S59. *PDS.*

Right: RICCARTON: No. 37080 shunts 46-tonne oil tanks at Riccarton, prior to departure with 6N61, the 1515 Mondays-only 'empties' to Grangemouth, July 11 1988. *PDS.*

Left: IRVINE: Class 37 No. 37023 reverses into the Down sidings at Irvine with 'trip' working R02 on July 12 1988. The load comprises four TTA tanks with caustic soda from Runcorn to Stevenston, and seven OTAs with timber from Fort William which will be detached here for Caberboard. The nearest OTA has round-topped ends which betray its origins as a VDA van. *PDS.*

Mill at Barassie will bring at least two additional freight flows on to BR metals. One will be bulk china clay from Burngullow (Cornwall), conveyed in a twice-weekly block train of 14 purpose-built 100 tonne tanks and hauled by twin Class 37 locomotives. This will be the block train covering the longest distance on the BR system. The other flow will be timber from the West Highland Line,

Above: ANNBANK: The 1147 Knockshinnoch-Ayr Harbour coal train passes Annbank on July 13 1988, headed by Class 20s Nos. 20227 and 20192. On the right is the Killoch branch, access to which is controlled by the ground frame (in the foreground), which is released from Mauchline signal box. *PDS.*

conveyed by the daily Mossend - Falkland *Speedlink* service (6R43). These two traffics are expected to commence in early 1989.

GLASGOW

THE *Speedlink* distribution depot at Deanside is one of the jewels in the *Railfreight* crown north of the border. Established during the Second World War by the Canadian airforce, the depot was taken over by Clyde Navigation and then the Port of Clyde authority before it came under the ownership of J.G. Russell, who has run the facilities since 1983. The depot comprises four sheds each with 50,000 square feet of warehouse space. This rail served facility handles a constellation of products for distribution to the Glaswegian hinterland. Deanside Transit also own four ex-BR Class 08 shunting locomotives which handle the traffic within the terminus. These are Nos. 08292/345/728/736, all maintained under contract by BR but operated and owned by Deanside.

Railfreight have two methods of delivery to Deanside. *Speedlink* 'trip' service T56, based at Polmadie, shuttles between Mossend and Deanside three times each day. In addition there is a direct service between Deanside and Wisbech to deal with the Spillers pet food traffic (6L80, the 1552

Above: DEANSIDE TRANSIT: Class 08 No. 08728 propels a VGA van with timber from Cardiff docks and an empty *Minilink* container wagon while privately-owned Class 08 No. 08292 awaits its next duty at Deanside. In the centre distance (alongside the 'Deanside Transit' shed) Class 08 No.08736 stands with ferry vans being loaded with whisky for Spain. Out of sight behind the central warehouse is Class 08 No.08345, shunting the Wisbech train.This picture was taken on July 26 1988. *MR.*

Deanside-Wisbech). *Freightliner* traffic is easily 'roaded' from either Coatbridge or Gushetfaulds and many maritime containers deliver goods from all over the world. A visit to Deanside in July 1988 revealed the following traffic in the sidings and warehouses: timber in VGA vans from Cardiff and Avonmouth docks, for a local furnished kitchen company. Bulmer's cider from Hereford for sale in local supermarkets and pubs had arrived on 6S74, from Cardiff Tidal to Mossend. The 6S73 Dover-Mossend had delivered ferry wagons containing Yugoslavian washing powder and shot-blast (for cleaning steel) from West Germany. Other *Speedlink* traffic included paper from

Left: *MINILINK*: A *Minilink* container awaits departure from Deanside with shampoo destined for local supermarkets. The container was transferred from rail to road in a matter of two minutes. *MR.*

Below: ROTHESAY DOCK: Class 26 Nos. 26004 and 26007 propel empty HEA wagons into the loading area at Rothesay dock, having arrived with the 6Z63, the 1005 Kincardine-Rothesay service. HEA hoppers were used on the run to Kincardine because the automatic discharge apparatus at the power station had been out of use for three years and needed servicing. HAA hoppers can be used on trips to Longannet and Cockenzie. *PDS.*

Hartlepool and Shotton for local newspapers, empty cans for Spillers dog food, from Wisbech, and milling wheat from East Anglia, for grading. This last traffic was at a low ebb in 1988 because of a poor harvest.

Lambrusco wine arrives via Tilbury and travels by *Freightliner* to Coatbridge. A fascinating cargo of Chinese peanuts for human consumption was also found in one corner of the warehouse. These had arrived via the *Freightliner* from Felixstowe accompanied by Pakistani cloth for a local clothing factory. Further avenues are being explored with the introduction of the *Minilink* container system on the run between Willesden and Deanside Transit. To date, customers have ranged from a prominent shampoo manufacturer to a fuse wire company! The enterprise

of J.G. Russell has allowed Deanside to absorb the majority of traffic previously dealt with at Sighthill, Glasgow High Street and Paisley Underwood goods depots.

Glasgow has its own *Freightliner* depot at Gushetfaulds. Five departures each day serve UK destinations; most maritime traffic travels via Coatbridge. Departures from Gushetfaulds are as follows:- 4M83, the 0125 (MX) to Willesden; 4M44, the 0700 (SO) to Trafford Park; 4D31, the 1845 (SX) to Coatbridge; 4M89, the 2120 (SX) to Willesden; and 4M51, the 2240 (SX) to Basford Hall.

Speedlink traffic on the north bank of the Clyde is dealt with by *Speedlink* trip diagrams N22 and N24. These service the fuel depot at Bowling, which receives gas oil by

Right: GUSHETFAULDS: No. 47249 positions its train under the unloading crane at Gushetfaulds after arriving with 4S89, the 0425 Willesden-Gushetfaulds *Freightliner* service. On July 13 1988, a wide variety of containers can be seen in the yard, including whisky tanks on the right. *PDS.*

Below: SIGHTHILL: On July 14 1988, the 1140 Corpach-Mossend service (7D19) is seen passing the sight of the old goods depot at Sighthill. Class 37 No. 37423 heads six empty TTA fuel tanks and two FGA *Freightliner* vehicles carrying paper from Corpach to Wiggins Teape in Cardiff, as mentioned on page 134. *PDS.*

Right: PAISLEY HAWKHEAD BRANCH: The branch to Hawkhead oil terminal sees a twice weekly fuel train from Grangemouth which delivers fuel for Glasgow airport. On July 13 1988, the 1540 Hawkhead-Grangemouth empty oil service (6N55) is seen approaching Corkerhill, half-way along the branch. The same locomotive diagram is used to deliver oil to Prestwick airport, near Ayr, when the Hawkhead service does not run. *PDS.*

GLASGOW AREA TRIP FREIGHTS FROM AUGUST 1988

CODE	LOCO	FROM (TIME)	TO (TIME)	TRAFFIC	DAYS
N22	26	Eastfield (1335)	Dalmuir (1400)	LE	SX
		Dalmuir (1420)	Dumbarton (1510)	Speedlink (Whisky)	SX
		Dumbarton (1555)	Mossend (1700)	Speedlink	SX
		Mossend (1805)	Bowling (1903)	Speedlink (Oil)	SX Y
		Bowling (1945)	Eastfield (2025)	Speedlink	SX Y
N24	26	Eastfield (0533)	Mossend (0603)	Speedlink	SX
		Mossend (0650)	Dumbarton (0803)	Speedlink (Whisky)	SX
		Dumbarton (0813)	Dalmuir (0855)	Speedlink	SX
		Dalmuir (0905)	Eastfield (0925)	LE	SX
		Eastfield (1010)	Mossend (1100)	Speedlink (Gas oil)	SX
		Mossend (1125)	Eastfield (1200)	Speedlink (Gas oil)	SX
N25	08	Cowlairs CS pilot			daily
N26	08	Glasgow loco works pilot			SX
T56	37	Mossend (0700)	Deanside (0805)	Speedlink	SX
		Deanside (0835)	Mossend (0930)	Speedlink	SX
		Mossend (1030)	Deanside (1130)	Speedlink	SX
		Deanside (1308)	Mossend (1408)	Speedlink	SX
		Mossend (1455)	Deanside (1606)	Speedlink	SX
		Deanside (1742)	Mossend (1845)	Speedlink	SX
T61	08	Polmadie pilot			daily

The following diagrams exist for departmental traffic:-

CODE	LOCO	FROM (TIME)	DAYS
N12	2x20	Eastfield AME instructions (tows electric units for maintenance)	SuX
N13	26	Glasgow Queen St (2200) ACE instructions, Cadder or Shettleston ballast	SO
N14	26	Glasgow Queen St (2129) ACE instructions, Cadder or Shettleston ballast	SO
N15	26	Eastfield (2330) ACE instructions	FX
N18	26	Eastfield (0810) ACE instructions	SX
N20	26	Eastfield (2320) AME instructions (overhead maintenance train)	SX
N21	37	Cadder (0618) ACE instructions (West Highland ballast)	SX Y
N23	37/4	Glasgow Queen St (004l) AME instructions	MO
N27	26	Eastfield (1025) ACE instructions	SX
N28	2x20	Eastfield (0815) RS &TE instructions (Yoker resignalling)	WFX
N29	any	Eastfield (2240) RS & TE instructions (Yoker resignalling)	SO
N30	2z20	Eastfield (2245) RS & TE instructions (Yoker resignalling)	SO
T52	26	Polmadie (0700), (1415), (2310) ACE instructions	SuX
T54	26	Polmadie (2345) AME instructions (overhead line maintenance)	SX/Sun
T57	26	Polmadie (2305) ACE instructions (Hillhouse quarry)	SX
T58	26	Polmadie (0900) ACE instructions	SX
T59	26	Polmadie (2300) ACE instructions	SO
T62	26	Polmadie (2330) ACE instructions	SO
T63	As available	Polmadie (2340) ACE instructions	SO

ship and despatches it by rail to Oban and Mallaig. The second terminal on the line is at Dalmuir Riverside, which receives whisky from Chivas at Keith. Coal traffic from Rothesay dock has greatly boosted the freight traffic passing Yoker. The line from Rothesay dock is connected to the carriage sidings at Yoker. Trains are booked to leave Rothesay at 1008 and 1830. These were initially sent to Kincardine power station, but following industrial unrest have now been diverted to either Longannet or Cockenzie. By August 1988, just 25,000 tons of coal had been railed to SSEB power stations; a total tonnage of one million tons is expected by the end of 1989. Mossend 'trip' 19 delivers goods to the *Speedlink* depots at Lugton (UKF fertiliser) and Giffen (government stores). 'Trips' T10 and T11 service Greenock Ladyburn and Bishopton. Ladyburn is owned by United Molasses who despatch to various Scottish customers, including Distillers at Menstrie (see page 117) and a distillery near Inverurie. The sidings at Bishopton handle government stores. One final rail head in the Glasgow area is the oil depot at Paisley Hawkhead which receives a twice weekly train from Grangemouth.

Right: GIFFEN : This delightful branch-line scene near Giffen depicts Class 37 No. 37251 with a single OAA barrier wagon, returning from Giffen to Mossend yard. The wagon will await further use at Mossend and may travel to act as a barrier wagon between the locomotive and any dangerous or noxious cargo. *PDS.*

Above: LUGTON: The 6T19 trip from Mossend is seen backing into the siding at Lugton, on July 15 1988. The guard will detach the rear ten OCA wagons, which contain bagged fertilizer from Ince and Elton, before the locomotive continues to Giffen with government stores. Class 37 No.37251 is in charge. *PDS.*

FREIGHT ONLY

MOTHERWELL

THE administrative centre for the majority of *Railfreight* activity in Scotland is based at Motherwell, where Area Manager John Clarke oversees activity in the central belt of Scotland. The operational centre for *Speedlink* traffic is just two miles north of Motherwell, at Mossend yard. A further two miles north lies Scotland's major *Freightliner* terminal at Coatbridge. Motherwell is therefore the focus for a great deal of freight traffic and has a *Railfreight* dedicated locomotive depot to provide motive power for the services in the area.

Mossend is a flat-shunted marshalling yard with 24 through sorting sidings on the Up side of the Coatbridge-Motherwell mainline. Three Class 08 shunting locomotives marshall traffic generated by more than 50 daily *Speedlink* workings and up to 20 local 'trip' workings (see accompanying tables). In addition, there are more than 40 block train services which utilize the yard for a variety of reasons. Some simply require a crew change, whilst trains from Hunterston to

Above: MOSSEND UP RECEPTION SIDINGS: In July 1988, coal began to travel by rail from Rothesay Dock to Kincardine power station. On July 26 1988, coal from Rothesay Dock had to be diverted to Cockenzie power station because of a dispute at Kincardine about the use of imported coal. On that day, a trainload of coal in HAA hoppers was stabled at Mossend after being brought from Rothesay by Class 37 No. 37403 and Class 26 No. 26002. It is seen here repositioned in the Up reception sidings by *Network South East* Class 86 No. 86401, which had just arrived at Mossend with a northbound Motorail service. *MR.*

Ravenscraig attach a banking engine for their journey up to the BSC plant. Some loads are staged in the yard, whilst others are split for distribution to local customers.

On the Down side of the line at Mossend are two rail-linked freight terminals. The first is owned by P.D. Stirling and handles a variety of bulk products for distribution to an area of about thirty miles radius, centred on Mossend. The site of the terminal allows easy access for wagons from Mossend yard which are delivered by the yard pilot engine. A six-month survey of traffic arriving at P.D.

Right: MOSSEND NORTH JUNCTION: Nos. 37370 and 37379 swing across the main line into No.1 Up Reception with 6S83, the Clitheroe-Gunnie cement train, on July 26 1988. The train conveyed ten tanks instead of the booked nine (see text). *MR.*

Right: MOSSEND YARD: An overall view of Mossend yard on July 26 1988 shows a wide variety of *Speedlink* wagons in the sidings. The Area Freight Centre is in the middle distance to the left of the picture and behind it is the cooling tower of BSC Ravenscraig. On the right is Class 37 No.37080 at the head of 6S36, the Dalston-Grangemouth. No. 37373 (the T17 pilot) and 26027 are also visible. *MR.*

Stirling highlights the wide variety of commodities handled by the three sidings at this depot. Steel arrived from Cardiff Tidal, Lackenby, Scunthorpe, Etruria and Sheerness. China clay from Marsh Mills, Goonbarrow, Burngullow, Trelavour and Heathfield was delivered by rail for distribution to the local paper and ceramics industries. Coal from South Wales and Yorkshire arrives by rail for use by both industrial and domestic customers. Bulk wagons containing lime arrive from Hindlow and 100 ton TEA

MOTHERWELL AREA TRIP FREIGHT SERVICES FROM AUGUST 1988
TRAINS FROM MOSSEND YARD

CODE	LOCO	TIME	TO (ARRIVAL TIME IN BRACKETS)	TRAFFIC	DAYS
T07	37	1503	Law Junc (1557) Mossend (1635)	Speedlink	SX
TO9	08		Ravenscraig No.3 pilot	Steel	SuX
T10	26	0718	Bishopton (0802), Ladyburn (0910), Mossend (1303)	Speedlink	SX
T11	26	1338	Ladyburn (1438), Bishopton (1540), Mossend (1742)	Speedlink	SX
T12	37/4	0825	Coltness (0855, Mossend (1015)	Departmental	SX
T14	37	0800	AFC Instructions (priority to Railfreight Metals)	Steel	SX
T16	37/3	0855	Ravenscraig No2 & No 4 pilot	Coal/Iron ore	SX
T17	37/3	1545	Ravenscraig No 2 & No 4 pilot	Coal/iron ore	SX
T18	37/3	2335	Ravenscraig No 2 & No 4 pilot	Coal/iron ore	SX
T19	37	0610	AFC instructions (priority to Gunnie traffic)	Cement	SX
		0845	Lugton/Giffen (0940), Mossend (21230)	Speedlink	SX Y
T25	08		Mossend South End pilot	Speedlink	SuX
T26	08		Mossend North End pilot	Speedlink	SuX
T29	08		Motherwell/Mossend pilot	Speedlink/ Departmental	SuX
T30	47	0935	Hamilton (0955), Mossend (1130)		
			Gartcosh (1240), St Rollox (1335), Mossend (1500)	Speedlink	SX

tankers carrying nitrogen travel from Ditton. Smaller consignments passing through include fruit, machinery, bricks and steel ingots from the continent. Aluminium arrives from Fort William, government stores from Trecwn and elsewhere and finally, there have been consignments of soft drinks from Wolverton and Ripple Lane. Such a wide variety of traffic can now be handled competitively because of the increased efficiency of *Speedlink* to deliver goods over 200 miles and the close proximity of P.D. Stirling to Mossend yard. British Rail also benefits from the overhead crane at the P.D. Stirling depot, which can be used to reposition loads on wagons if they have slipped during their journey to Mossend yard.

The second private siding at Mossend belongs to the Delta Coal company, which operates a small domestic coal depot at Mossend, receiving HEA hoppers of coal from South Wales and Yorkshire. The company has also recently negotiated the contract to handle imported coal at Rothesay Dock which has led to an upsurge in MGR traffic at Mossend yard.

To the south of Mossend lies BSC Ravenscraig, opened in 1956 and capable of producing 45,000 tons of molten steel each week. Current output is mainly in the form of hot rolled coil (HRC) which is distributed almost exclusively by rail. *Railfreight* operations at Ravenscraig are spread around four yards numbered in the order of their construction. No. 1 yard, the oldest, was originally used to marshal finished steel before departure. This role has now been taken over by No. 3 yard. No.1 yard now handles predominantly scrap traffic from Ravenscraig to local merchants, including Inshaw works in Motherwell. No. 2 yard was the arrival point for all raw materials when the works opened. It now handles only coal, which arrives from Hunterston coal terminal four times each weekday. No.3 yard is the site where trainloads of HRC are made up before despatch via Mossend yard to either Shotton or South Wales. There are three daily trains to Dee Marsh for Shotton and two services to Cardiff Tidal yard for distribution to Ebbw Vale, Velindre or Trostre. These carry a total of 25,000 tons of HRC each week. The most

Below: MOSSEND YARD NORTH EXIT: On April 24 1986, Class 20s Nos. 20171 and 20175 accelerate north with 7N23, the 1050 Mossend-Grangemouth service. In 1988 this particular service no longer runs, but Grangemouth is still served by two daily *Speedlink* services from Mossend. *MR.*

TRUNK FREIGHT SERVICES FROM MOSSEND YARD ROM AUGUST 1988

CODE	FROM	TO	ARR	DEP	PASS	TRAFFIC	DAYS
6M61	Gunnie	Clitheroe	0010	0012		Cement	MO
6S79	Oakleigh	Larbert	0026	0030		Chemicals	TThO
6D02	Inverness	Mossend	0040			Speedlink	MX
6S43	Grimethorpe	Mossend	0043			Speedlink Coal	MO
7D10	Corpach	Mossend	0044			Speedlink	MX
7N53	Mossend	Grangemouth		0050		Speedlink	MX
6S47	Dee Marsh	Mossend	0102			Steel	MX
6S67	Healey Mills	Gartcosh	0109	0135		Speedlink Coal	MX
7D12	Hunterston	Ravenscraig	0116	0133		Coal*	MX
6S58	Ellesmere Port	Mossend	0129			Speedlink	MX
6M25	Mossend	Dee Marsh		0137		Steel	SX
6S80	Warrington WOJ	Mossend	0153			Speedlink	MX
9D37	Millerhill	Mossend	0212			Departmental	MX
6S73	Dover	Mossend	0224			Speedlink	MX
6S53	Carlisle NY	Grangemouth			0248	Oil	MThX
4S52	Willesden	Coatbridge			0257	Freightliner	MX
9B78	Mossend	Millerhill		0303		Departmental	MX
7E34	Gartcosh	Healey Mills	0328	0410		Speedlink coal	MX
6D30	Hunterston	Ravenscraig	0347	0404		Iron Ore*	MX
6D49	Grangemouth	Mossend	0403			Speedlink	MX
6S81	Tyne	Mossend	0410			Speedlink	MX
4S81	Pengam	Coatbridge			0446	Freightliner	MX
6D03	Craiginches	Mossend	0453			Speedlink	MX
4S83	Tilbury	Coatbridge			0455	Freightliner	MX
6D32	Hunterston	Ravenscraig	0509	0528		Iron ore*	MX
6M24	Mossend	Dee Marsh		0525		Steel	SX
7N51	Mossend	Grangemouth		0530		Speedlink	MX
6S57	Sheerness	Mossend	0534			Speedlink	MX
6M34	Grangemouth	Dalston			0540	Oil	WSX
6S74	Cardiff Tidal	Mossend	0605			Speedlink	MX
6S82	Bescot	Mossend	0620			Speedlink	MX
6V75	Mossend	Cardiff Tidal		0635		Steel	MX
6D03	Fort William	Mossend	0729			Alumina	MX
6S71	Whitemoor	Mossend	0729			Speedlink	MX
7V93	Mossend	Stoke Gifford		0730		Speedlink	SX
6V39	Mossend	Margam		0736		Steel	SO
6M27	Larbert	Oakleigh	0700	0740		Chemicals	SO
4D45	Coatbridge	Motherwell			0748	Freightliner	MSX
7D07	Hunterston	Ravenscraig	0743	0759		Coal*	SO
4D46	Coatbridge	Mossend	0750			Freightliner	SO
4S80	Felixstowe	Coatbridge			0759	Freightliner	MX
6B64	Mossend	Millerhill		0805		Speedlink	MX
6A19	Mossend	Aberdeen		0805		Speedlink	MX
4O81	Coatbridge	Southampton	0805	0810		Freightliner	SO
6D27	Grangemouth	Wishaw			0817	Oil	TO
6E46	Mossend	Blyth Dock		0840		Alumina	SX
6S96	Parkeston	Mossend	0844			Speedlink	MX
4D47	Mossend	Motherwell		0859		Freightliner	MO
6V39	Mossend	Cardiff Tidal		0910		Steel	MSX
7Y39	Mossend	Oban		0945		Speedlink	MWFO Y
7Y41	Mossend	Arrochar		0945		Speedlink	TThO Y
7N67	Mossend	Stirling		1002		Speedlink	SX
6D08	Hunterston	Ravenscraig	1006	1021		Iron ore*	SuX
6M23	Mossend	Dee Marsh		1120		Steel	SX
6S75	Warrington WOJ	Mossend	1121			Speedlink	MX
7S53	Hardendale	Mossend	1145			Limestone	SX
4S89	Willesden	Coatbridge	1150	1152		Freightliner	SO
7Y37	Mossend	Mallaig Junc		1152		Speedlink	SX
7D09	Hunterston	Ravenscraig	1208	1223		Coal*	SuX
6M63	Mossend	Carlisle		1236		Limestone	SuX
6S56	Blyth	Mossend	1247			Alumina	SX
6D11	Hunterston	Ravenscraig	1254	1309		Iron Ore*	SuX
6D26	Grangemouth	Mossend	1345			Speedlink	SX
6S42	Dee Marsh	Mossend	1408			Steel	SX
6N59	Wishaw	Grangemouth	1402	1407		Oil	TO Y
6L97	Mossend	Ripple Lane		1440		Speedlink	SX
6S51	Llandarcy	Grangemouth	1517	1519		Oil	WFO
7S97	Gloucester	Mossend	1559			Speedlink	MSX
7S97	Bescot	Mossend	1559			Speedlink	MO

Table continued on opposite page......

TRUNK FREIGHT SERVICES FROM MOSSEND YARD FROM AUGUST 1988

CODE	FROM	TO	ARR	DEP	PASS	TRAFFIC	DAYS
6M27	Larbert	Oakleigh	1550	1635		Chemicals	TO
7D23	Oban	Mossend	1607			Speedlink	MWFO Y
7D23	Arrochar	Mossend	1607			Speedlink	TThO Y
6V92	Mossend	Tavistock Junc		1610		Speedlink	SX
6L80	Deanside	Wisbech			1650	Speedlink	SX
7D13	Hunterston	Ravenscraig	1643	1703		Coal*	SX
6S36	Dalston	Grangemouth	1644	1653		Oil	WSX
4D44	Motherwell	Coatbridge			1727	Freightliner	SX
6D14	Hunterston	Ravenscraig	1757	1817		Iron ore*	SX
4V63	Coatbridge	Pengam			1815	Freightliner	SX
6M64	Craiginches	Willesden	1821	2000		Speedlink	SX
7D19	Corpach	Mossend	1830			Speedlink	SX
6D20	Falkland Junc	Mossend	1839			Speedlink	SX
6D48	Millerhill	Mossend	1854			Speedlink	SX
6B68	Inverness	Millerhill	1856	2020		Speedlink	SX
6S50	Dee Marsh	Mossend	1857			Steel	SX
6L86	Mossend	Whitemoor		1920		Speedlink	SX
6D21	Grangemouth	Mossend	1928			Speedlink	SX
4L81	Coatbridge	Stratford			1950	Freightliner	SX
7Y31	Mossend	Mallaig Junc		1950		Speedlink	SX
6V53	Grangemouth	Llandarcy			1957	Oil	MWO
6M79	Mossend	Bescot		2025		Speedlink	SX
6M38	Grangemouth	Carlisle NY			2028	Oil	WSX
6D24	Hunterston	Ravenscraig	2013	2132		Iron Ore*	SX
6S83	Clitheroe	Gunnie	2011	2030		Cement	SX
6S60	Coedbach	Mossend	2037			Speedlink Coal	SO
4L95	Coatbridge	Felixstowe			2046	Freightliner	SX
6H31	Mossend	Inverness		2059		Speedlink	SX
4L97	Coatbridge	Felixstowe	2107	2109		Freightliner	SX
7N69	Mossend	Grangemouth		2112		Speedlink	SX
6M28	Mossend	Willesden		2115		Speedlink	SX
6R43	Mossend	Falkland Junc		2202		Speedlink	SX
6M83	Mossend	Warrington Arp		2205		Speedlink	SX
6D25	Hunterston	Ravenscraig	2222	2242		Iron Ore*	SX
6M61	Mossend	Clitheroe		2310		Cement	FSX
6Y35	Mossend	Fort William		2318		Alumina	SX
4S59	Southampton	Coatbridge			2324	Freightliner	FO
6A17	Mossend	Craiginches		2334		Speedlink	SX
6D22	Grangemouth	Mossend	2353			Speedlink	SX

* These services pause at Mossend to attach banking assistance for the climb to Ravenscraig

modern yard, No. 4, is the arrival point for iron ore, limestone and dolophines. Iron ore arrives from the Hunterston terminal seven times each weekday. Limestone is transported from Hardendale quarry, at Shap, by a daily block load known locally as the 'white ladies' because of the characteristic lime staining on the wagons. A second flux for the steel-making process arrives daily from Thrislington in county Durham. This dolophine traffic has caused British Rail some headaches because of its powdery nature. One fur-coated lady on Berwick station is known to have asked for damages when the 0905 Thrislington-Ravenscraig No.4 (6S54) thundered through Berwick station and caused damage to her fur coat; the outcome of the case is awaited at the time of going to press! Such a minor setback is unlikely to jeopardise this traffic; it was won for rail four years ago when J.G. Russell

started to carry the dolophines in their distinctive silver FPA container wagons. At that stage, the traffic was delivered to the J.G. Russell distribution depot at Gartcosh and transported by road to Ravenscraig. Introduction of PTA tippler wagons in 1987 has led to direct rail delivery to Ravenscraig.

Adjacent to the BSC complex at Ravenscraig are two further BSC plants. BSC Dalzell is connected by a BSC railway to Ravenscraig whilst BSC Clydesdale is served by British Rail. At Clydesdale, steel tubes and pipes are manufactured. Tubes are sent for finishing to BSC Imperial and travel on the T14 'trip.' This traffic is sporadic and dependent upon orders for such pipes. At the time of writing an upsurge in this traffic was expected.

A description of the daily work of trip freights from Mossend yard will help to explain the many and varied connections between *Railfreight* and local industry. All

Right: P.D. STIRLING: On July 26 1988, the sidings at the P.D. Stirling depot are well stocked with high capacity *Speedlink* wagons. On the right, china clay and lime await unloading. Piles of steel wire from Cardiff are stacked against the warehouse wall. *MR.*

Mossend trip freights are listed in the table on page 102.

'Trip' T07 services the Isis Link distribution depot at Law Junction. This depot was the first privately-owned general goods depot in Scotland and is sited so far south of Glasgow because at the time it was feared that it might take traffic away from BR goods depots like Glasgow High Street. In 1988, the situation has turned full circle, with BR anxious to co-operate wherever possible with private companies who wish to set up rail-served goods depots. Law Junction receives traffic from the 6S96 freight each morning, which calls on its way north. The T07 'trip' travels just once each day to pick up empty wagons. Regular traffics handled are Campbells soups from King's Lynn, Taunton cider and bricks from Butterley; occasional loads of refined industrial sand also travel to Law in palletised form. These travel in VAA vans from King's Lynn. Industrial raw materials have arrived from Hallen Marsh and until recently fertilizer was handled. This traffic is

Right: RAVENSCRAIG NO. 1: On April 24 1986, Class 20 No. 20127 stands in No.1 yard at the head of a load of scrap en route from Ravenscraig to Shieldmuir, via Mossend. The 'trip' is T12, which has already travelled to Coltness and has been allocated to fill in on a Metals sector turn. It is more usual for T14 to deal with this traffic. *MR.*

Above: RAVENSCRAIG NO. 2: Class 37s Nos. Nos. 37310 *British Steel Ravenscraig* and 37190 have just arrived at No. 2 yard with 7D09 from Hunterston Coal Terminal. The blast furnaces of BSC Ravenscraig dominate the background. *MR.*

now dealt with at Leith. The Isis Link terminal was previously owned by Cory and under this ownership was the first depot to carry Spillers petfood by rail. In the 1970s, it was transported from Law to the BR goods depot at King's Lynn from where it was 'roaded' to Wisbech. A more direct passage was afforded when Spillers were able to load wagons at Paisley Underwood, but this arrangement suffered because of the lack of covered accommodation at Paisley. Three years ago, this traffic was transferred to Deanside transit which had been taken over by J.G. Russell and the goods now travel directly from this depot to Wisbech. The T07 operates the remainder of its eight-hour shift according to the instructions of the Area Freight Centre, with priority being given to Gunnie traffic.

T10 and T11 both serve the same pair of railheads at Greenock Ladyburn and Bishopton. These are dealt with in the Glasgow section of the book. T12 visits Coltness each day to pick up concrete sleepers. The depot at Coltness produces various concrete beams which are used in bridge building. T19 'trips' to Gunnie on a regular basis, but may also fill in on other turns if required.

The Gunnie factory is far more than simply a cement terminal. Portland cement is delivered from Clitheroe, 60% of it by rail. This traffic has been won back by BR in spite of ruthless competition from road haulage companies who contribute nothing to their transport infrastructure. A novel operational arrangement allows 13 tanks of cement to be delivered each day to Gunnie. The train of 13 tanks (which weighs 1300) tons is split at Carlisle with nine tanks continuing as a block load to Gunnie. This allows diesel haulage over Beattock. The remaining four tanks travel north to Mossend on a *Speedlink* service and are then 'tripped' to

Right: RAVENSCRAIG NO. 3: Class 08 No. 08736 trundles through the murk and grime of No.3 yard with a single BBA steel wagon, which has just been loaded with hot rolled steel coil bound for Ebbw Vale. The yard also contains wagons of limestone from Hardendale, which in 1986 were delivered to the works via No.1 yard but now travel to No.4 yard. *MR.*

Above: RAVENSCRAIG NO. 4: On April 12 1986, Class 37 Nos. 37099 and 37037 ease forward from the No. 4 yard wagon tippler, which has just unloaded 1,500 tons of iron ore in a little over 15 minutes. They will now head the 6J05 service back to Hunterston iron-ore terminal. *MR.*

Gunnie. The cement is then processed into eleven different grades before distribution to customers all over Scotland. Castle Cement, which owns the Gunnie factory, also have rail terminals at Dundee, Aberdeen and Inverness. These do not see any traffic at the time of writing but may well begin to receive cement by rail before the end of 1988. The cement factory at Gunnie occupies the site of Scotland's first railway, which carried mineral traffic from the area to the Forth and Clyde canal. The area around Gunnie once contained more than 30 blast furnaces, known collectively as the Gartsherrie iron works. The second job of the day for T19 is

to visit Lugton and Giffen; these railheads are described in the Glasgow chapter.

T30 has a busy day, with responsibility for shunting E.G. Steele and Tennants at Hamilton in the morning. A lunchtime 'trip' is then made to J.G. Russell, at Gartcosh. This is predominantly a coal trans-shipment point. More than 200,000 tons of coal are handled each year, from pits in Yorkshire and South Wales. The Gartcosh site also houses container repair facilities and coal stocks. A regular single container of whisky is delivered to Gartcosh from Invergordon (See page 109) but otherwise coal is the sole commodity at this depot. The T30 'trip' must

Above: GARTCOSH: 6T74 (now coded 6T30) from Gartcosh (Russells) to Mossend yard is seen passing Gartcosh Junction on April 24 1986. Class 27 No. 27042 is hauling four empty FPA coal containers and a single tank returning to the M.K. Shand distillery, in Invergordon. In the background are the BSC Gartcosh works, which had closed a few weeks earlier. *MR.*

Above: COATBRIDGE *FREIGHTLINER* TERMINAL: In a midday thunderstorm on July 16 1988, Class 37s Nos. 37053 & 37055 stand in the *Freightliner* depot at Coatbridge. They have arrived on the 4S80 service from Felixstowe, hauling maritime containers, and will return to East Angia later in the evening. *MR.*

return to Mossend via Sighthill where it runs round. A visit may be made to St. Rollox if there are any spare parts from Crewe to deliver to the BR locomotive works.

The T14 'trip' has already been mentioned earlier in this chapter. In addition to its work between Clydesdale and Imperial it is also responsible for the carriage of scrap between Ravenscraig No.1 yard and Camlachie, St. Rollox, Shieldmuir and Mossend.

A second cement terminal in the Mother-well area is the Blue Circle terminal at Uddingston. This receives regular blockloads from Oxwellmains and occasionally

Right: GARNQUEEN NORTH JUNCTION On July 26 1988, Class 37 Nos. 37191 and 37188 travel south through the pouring rain at the head of 6N70, the 1351 Grangemouth-Bishopbriggs oil train. *MR.*

despatches bagged cement in VDA vans. Ten trains a week, each carrying 740 tons of cement in PCA tanks mean that nearly 250,000 tons of cement pass through Uddingston's four 1200-ton capacity silos each year! Imagine how many lorries that keeps of the roads. If there is any spare capacity in the PCA pool then wagons may be used to ship cement from Uddingston to Ayr Harbour, from where it is exported to Ireland.

The final major rail terminal in the area is the *Freightliner* depot at Coatbridge. The services to and from Coatbridge may be found in the Mossend table. It is of interest that transfer of containers from road to rail and rail to rail takes place at Coatbridge. Railborne pulp from Corpach is delivered in containers on FPA *Freightliner* wagons and is then transferred to the Pengam bound set of wagons for carriage down to Cardiff.

The Motherwell area is a prosperous one for *Railfreight.* There are prospects of new

Above: GUNNIE BRANCH: Class 26 No. 26027 eases along the Gunnie branch with the T07 trip on July 26 1988, when the train was recoded 7Z01, because of rearrangements in the timetable to cater for the Glasgow and Motherwell holidays. The six empty cement tanks will return to Mossend yard and then south to Clitheroe. *MR.*

Left: ABINGTON: The splendid scenery of the Lowther Hills forms the backdrop for Class 85 No. 85021 as it speeds south with 6V92, the 1610 Mossend-Gloucester service. The train consists of a single PBA returning to Cornwall, 5 OBAs, 1 TEA, 1 BDA, 2 PFBs, 1 VEA, 2 VGAs and a rake of 20 VEA vans containing government stores. *PDS.*

Above: LAW JUNCTION: The distribution depot at Law Junction handles a variety of commodities ranging from soup to bricks and cider. On July 26 1988, Class 26 No. 26027 eases three PVA vans bound for King's Lynn, out of the depot for the trip to Mossend. *MR.*

Left: GUNNIE CEMENT WORKS: One of the privately-owned industrial shunting locomotives at Gunnie draws past the storage silos at the plant with two empty cement tanks. After weighing on the electronic weighbridge, they will be taken to the BR exchange sidings for 'tripping' to Mossend. *MR.*

traffic from Gunnie and to BSC Imperial. A new MGR coal terminal at Ravenstruther near Carstairs will add further to *Railfreight* tonnages as it is due to despatch two trainloads of coal from the Dalquhandy opencast site to Ayr Docks each day. *Railfreight* is alive and well in Motherwell.

FIFE & CLACKMANNAN

RAILFREIGHT activity in the kingdom of Fife is centred on Thornton marshalling yard. This mechanised hump yard was built in the 1950s to cater principally for coal traffic in the area, but never saw full usage as the nearby Glenrothes pit was flooded before full coal production could begin. In 1988, a small collection of sidings handle coal and *Speedlink* traffic. *Speedlink* 'trip' freights visit several terminals in the area. The G14 pilot services the Auchmuty branch which winds west from Markinch to the Tullis paper mill. China clay from Cornwall is delivered at the rate of eight PAA wagons each week. Fife Paper Ltd lies half-way along the branch and receives a single ferry van of pulp each week. In late 1988, no paper was leaving by rail and the old flows of coal and Pampas grass are now memories. An occasional tank of CO_2 arrives for use at Tullis works, but pulp travels by road from Methil docks or Montrose. The branch is unique in possessing Britain's narrowest tunnel; there is just half an inch clearance for a Class 08 easing through the stone archway of this structure!

The G05 diagram services principally the Methil docks branch. At Methil docks there are sidings which handle pulp imported from Scandinavia. Shipments are made to Fort William for Corpach. The pulp is carried in VDA vans or the experimental OEA covered wagon. Traffic is variable and dependent upon orders for pulp from Methil. A more regular traffic is the grain flow to Cameron Bridge for the local distillery. This arrives daily in *Polybulk* wagons from East Anglia and is supplemented by tanks of CO_2 gas, used in distilling process.

Speedlink traffic is also picked up at Crombie and Rosyth docks where the RNAD have large depots. Crombie is served by the G05 trip whereas Rosyth is visited by the afternoon Thornton to Millerhill freight. The dockyard may also be serviced by a direct trip from Millerhill yard if necessary.

Coal is produced at two sites in Fife. The Longannet complex, which has reserves of 111 million tons, is not rail served and delivers all its output by conveyor to Longannet power station.

Above: THORNTON YARD: The 1340 Perth-Millerhill *Speedlink* (6B66) called at Thornton yard until its withdrawal from the timetable in 1987. On May 12 1986, Class 47 No. 47337 leads a varied load of empty wagons with two loaded OTA timber wagons at the rear. Traffic from Perth to Millerhill now travels on either the Inverness or Aberdeen services which call at Perth on their way south. Thornton despatches traffic to Millerhill on the afternoon 6B59 *Speedlink* 'trip.' The remains of the flooded Glenrothes pit can be seen in the background. In the middle distance stands Thornton yard signal cabin and the locomotive servicing point. *MR.*

In contrast to the new mine at Longannet, the opencast site at Westfield is nearing the end of its life. Coal stocks from Westfield are sent by rail to either Methil power station, which is specially designed to burn low grade slurry, or Longannet power station. The G01 'tripper' from Thornton spends two eight-hour shifts shuttling between Westfield and Methil whilst a second pair of Class 20 locomotives are responsible for the G12 turn to Longannet. Coal may arrive in Fife from the Edinburgh pits or from Rothesay docks. Such flows of coal are dependent upon the demand for fuel at Longannet and Kincardine power stations.

To the west of Fife is the county of Clackmannan. A short freight-only line runs beneath the Ochil hills from Stirling to Alloa. The Grangemouth trip diagram N06 travels from Mossend yard to Stirling, arriving in Stirling at 1057. The Class 37 then runs to Alloa (Cambus) and Menstrie as required.

Grain from East Anglia is delivered to the whisky distillery at Cambus whilst the factory at Menstrie receives molasses from York, King's Lynn and Greenock.

THORNTON YARD FREIGHT SERVICES FROM AUGUST 1988

CODE	LOCO	TIME	FROM	TO (ARR TIME IN BRACKETS)	TRAFFIC	DAYS
G01	2x20	0635	Thornton	Westfield (065)	LE	SX
		0725	Westfield	Methil (0825)	Coal	SX
		0910	Methil	Westfield (1125)	Coal	SX
		1220	Westfield	Methil (1315)	Coal	SX
		1400	Methil	Millerhill via Thornton (1537)	Speedlink	SX
		1610	Millerhill	Methil (1808)	LE	SX
		1853	Methil	Westfield (1935)	Coal	SX
		2040	Westfield	Thornton (2100)	LE	SX
6G43	26	0725	Millerhill	Thornton	Speedlink	SX
G05	26	0915	Thornton (Loco off 6G43)	AFC instructions:- priority to Cameron Bridge and Methil	Speedlink	SX
6G44	26	1042	Millerhill	Thornton	Speedlink	SX
G05		1255	Thornton	AFC instructions:- priority to Crombie, Cameron Bridge & Methil	Speedlink	SX
6G44		1330	Thornton	Rosyth & Millerhill (16.52)	Speedlink	SX
6B59		1525	Thornton (loco off G05)	Millerhill (16.45)	Speedlink	SX
G12	2x20	0635	Thornton	Westfield (07.13)	MGR	SX
		0828	Westfield	Longannet (10.08)	MGR	SX
		1048	Longannet	Westfield (12.15)	MGR	SX
		1330	Westfield	Longannet (15.00)	MGR	SX
		1546	Longannet	Thornton (16.33)	MGR	SX
G14	08	0700	Thornton pilot	Markinch/Auchmuty	Speedlink	SX

The following diagrams exist for departmental traffic:-

G10	20	0730	Thornton ACE instructions			SX
G16	26	2210	Thornton ACE instructions			SO
G17	2x26	2240	Thornton ACE instructions			SO

Left: THORNTON YARD : In 1980 the scene was very different at Thornton. The fuelling point had yet to receive its covered accommodation (right side of picture) and much unfitted freight traffic was still to be seen. On June 30 1980, Class 20 Nos. 20224 and 20221 wind out of the yard with a rake of empty HAA hoppers for Westfield opencast site. Here they will be loaded with coal for Longannet power station. *MR.*

Right: **AUCHMUTY:** On May 2 1986, Class 08 No. 08515 creeps along the Auchmuty branch with the morning 'trip' from Tullis paper mill to Markinch. The engine and brake van are about to squeeze through the narrowest tunnel on the route, with a clearance of just half an inch! *MR.*

Below: **METHIL POWER STATION:** Class 20s Nos. 20221 and 20224 turn into Methil power station on May 12 1986 with a load of twenty MDV wagons containing coal slurry from Westfield opencast site. At this time, the train was coded 6G02; this was changed to 6G01 in 1988. *MR.*

Above: **METHIL DOCKS:** On May 2 1986, Class 26 No. 26027 stands in the yard at Methil docks with the 6G01 'tripper' from Thornton yard. The sidings are full of air-braked vans loaded with imported pulp. The second vehicle behind the locomotive is an experimental conversion of an OBA open wagon. It is fitted with a removable roof and coded OEA. In 1988, this branch is served by the 6G05 trip freight with 6G01 being reallocated to carry traffic from Westfield. *MR.*

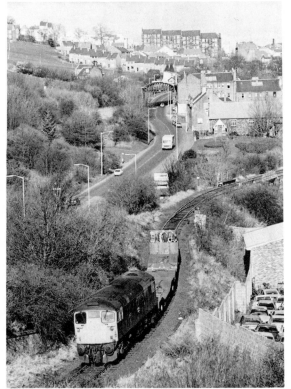

Top: INVERKEITHING: Much of the ballast for the rail-ways of SE Scotland is loaded at Inverkeithing. On March 1 1988, Class 26 No. 26043 heads south with 7B13, the Inverkeithing-Millerhill engineers duty. *MR.*

Above: CROMBIE: The branch to the RNAD depot at Crombie winds down to the sea through a densely wooded area. Despite five attempts, we have never managed to catch a train on this most picturesque line! The line from Dunfermline is on the right, the spur down to Crombie on the left. March 1 1988. *MR.*

Left: ROSYTH DOCK: The 6G44 departure from Thorn-ton yard calls at Rosyth naval yard on its way to Millerhill. On March 1 1988, No. 26021 is about to pass beneath the main line at Inverkeithing with two empty bogie bolster wagons and a single ODA, carrying lead piping. The engine continued light to Millerhill. *MR.*

Right: ALLOA YARD: The remains of the once-extensive yard at Alloa were used until 1988 to allow the Cambus trip freight to run round. The yard formerly served several local brewers and distilleries, as well as local mines and the docks at Alloa. Here, on May 12 1986 Class 27 No. 27059 runs round 6N06, the Grangemouth-Cambus *Speedlink* 'trip'. The first three wagons contain grain from Royston for the distillery at Cambus whilst the next eight are TTA tanks of molasses to Menstrie. In 1988, 6N06 runs from Mossend to Cambus and a new run-round loop has allowed the closure of Alloa Yard. *MR.*

Below: LONGANNET power station is seen in the background as Class 20 Nos. 20226 & 20201 tackle the gradient at Torry Bay, on the north of the Forth estuary, on March 1 1988. On this occasion, coal from Bilston Glen was diverted to Longannet instead of its normal destination at Cockenzie power station, and this is 7Z42, the Longannet-Bilston 'empties'. *MR.*

Above: MENSTRIE: Brooding skies and the Ochil hills watch over Class 27 No. 27059 as it arrives at Menstrie with eight tanks of molasses. They are from Kings Lynn, York and Greenock and travelled north via Mossend and Grangemouth yards. *MR.*

Left: WESTFIELD: Class 20s Nos. 20221 and 20224 snake out of the Westfield opencast site with the 6G02 'trip' to Methil power station. Although open cast mining has ceased at Westfield, in late 1988 there were large stocks of coal to be moved by rail to Methil and Longannet. *MR.*

EDINBURGH

Above: COCKENZIE: The B08 'trip' has just arrived at the unloading shed in Cockenzie power station on March 1 1988. Class 26 No. 26004 is leading a train of coal from the 400,000-tons stockpile at Monktonhall. *MR.*

MILLERHILL yard, to the south east of Edinburgh, was built as part of the 1955 modernisation plan and had both Up and Down humps with 80 sorting sidings. In 1988, just the southern end of the Up yard remains to handle *Speedlink* traffic in and around the Scottish capital.

The yard is in the process of modernisation as part of the East Coast Main Line electrification scheme and will receive a new name and identity during 1989. The trunk freight services to use the yard are listed on page 120, whilst trip freights are shown on page 121.

Coal traffic in the Edinburgh area is generated by the mine at Bilston Glen and the opencast site at Blindwells. A third railhead is the pit at Monktonhall, adjacent to the old Millerhill Down yard. The output from Monktonhall is stockpiled because of difficulty in selling coal to the local SSEB power stations. Imported coal, like that moved by rail from Rothesay dock, is considerably cheaper than Scottish deep-mined coal and the deep mines in Scotland are therefore under threat as coal imports increase. Trip diagrams B08, B09, B10 and B26 may be directed to Monktonhall if there is an order for its coal. Bilston Glen mine at Loanhead

produces more than one million tons of coal each year, and two-thirds of this goes to the local power generation industry. This translates into five MGR trainloads each day to Cockenzie, with occasional extra services to Longannet. The opencast site at Blindwells also produces three trainloads of coal each day for Cockenzie power station. The five million tons of coal at this site were due to run out during 1988, but the loading facilities may be retained to act as a disposal point for other opencast developments. A small opencast site was opened at Roughcastle, near Falkirk, in 1986 and 180,000 tons of coal will be extracted by 1989. Rail is used to carry the coal to Cockenzie or Longannet.

Domestic coal arrives in Edinburgh from Yorkshire on 6S67, the Healey Mills-Gartcosh *Speedlink Coal* service. Coal from Wales may also arrive via Mossend. Local distribution to Haymarket and Portobello coal concentration depots is undertaken by the B24 'trip' from Millerhill yard.

FREIGHT ONLY

Top: MILLERHILL YARD: On March 1 1988, the Methil Docks-Millerhill (7G01) arrives at Millerhill. On the right are the earthworks of the old Down hump yard, whilst on the left the TOPS office and diesel servicing depot can just be seen. No. 26014 is hauling a variety of empty wagons, including three empty CO2 tankers, a VEA van, a single PBA china clay carrier and two OTA timber vehicles. In May 1988, this freight was rediagrammed 6B59, Thornton-Millerhill, with an arrival time at Millerhill of 1545. *MR.*

Above: BILSTON GLEN: Class 26 No. 26005, one of a *Trainload Coal* dedicated fleet, stands at Bilston Glen exchange sidings on March 1 1988. Class 08 No. 08570 was on loan to British Coal at this stage and had just brought a rake of loaded HAA hoppers into the yard. No. 26005 will take them forward as 7B26, to Cockenzie power station. The train runs via the Monktonhall curve, avoiding Millerhill yard. *MR.*

CODE	FROM	TO	ARR	DEP	TRAFFIC	DAYS
9D37	Millerhill	Mossend		0001	Departmental	MX
6S63	Tees	Craiginches	2328	0028	SLK	MX
6S92	Scunthorpe	Craiginches	0224	0312	SLK	MX
6B86	View Park	Oxwellmains	0239	0523	cement	MX
6H25	Millerhill	Inverness		0345	SLK	MX
6S71	Whitemoor	Mossend	0537	0625	SLK	MX
4S39	Dagenham Dock	Millerhill	0753		oil	TThO
6N24	Leuchars	Grangemouth	0335	0505	cement	TThO
6B80	Grangemouth	Oxwellmains	0408	1040	departmental	MX
9B78	Mossend	Millerhill	0450		SLK coal	SX
7E34	Gartcosh	Healey Mills	0528	1434	cement	WFO
6B76	View Park	Oxwellmains	0557	1040	SLK	MSX
4B61	Mossend	Bathgate		0557	cement	MX
6B84	Craiginches	Oxwellmains	0653	0758	SLK	SO
4S48	Willesden	Bathgate	0705	1310	SLK	SX
6G43	Millerhill	Thornton		0703	cars	MX
4S64	Morris Cowley	Bathgate	0912	0916	SLK	MX
6B64	Mossend	Millerhill	0930		alumina	SX
6E46	Mossend	Blyth Dock	0952	1203	SLK	SX
4B62	Bathgate	Millerhill	1009		cement	MO
6B80	Millerhill	Oxwellmains		1040	SLK	SX
6G44	Millerhill	Thornton		1042	alumina	SX
6S56	Blyth Dock	Mossend	1053	1134	SLK coal	SX
6S46	Toton	Millerhill	1116		cement	SX
6B81	Oxwellmains	Millerhill	1305		SLK coal	SX
6E34	Millerhill	Healey Mills		1434	SLK	SX
4O38	Bathgate	Dover	1224	1448	limestone	SX
6S54	Thrislington	Ravenscraig	1440	1500	cars	MX
4M77	Bathgate	Washwood Hth	1501	1538	cars	MO
4M77	Millerhill	Washwood Hth		1538	SLK	SX
6L97	Mossend	Ripple Lane	1602	1707	SLK	SX
6D48	Millerhill	Mossend		1720	chemicals	TFO
8X98	Haverton Hill	Grangemouth	1611	1836	SLK	SX
6B59	Thornton	Millerhill	1645		oil	MWThO
6S62	Jarrow	Grangemouth	1719	1735	SLK	SX
6L87	Millerhill	Parkeston		1750	foodstuffs	FSX
6L80	Deanside	Wisbech	1801	1833	foodstuffs	FO
6L80	Deanside	Whitemoor	1801	1833	SLK	SX
6E89	Craiginches	Tyne	1843	1933	cement	SX
6D28	Oxwellmains	View Park	1916	1926	SLK coal	SX
6M17	Millerhill	Toton		2106	chemicals	MThO
8X99	Grangemouth	Haverton Hill	2058	2117	SLK	SX
6B68	Inverness	Millerhill	2137		oil	TWFO
6E58	Grangemouth	Jarrow	2149	2151	cement	MWFO
6N52	Oxwellmains	Grangemouth	2216	2321	cement	TThO
6D32	Oxwellmains	View Park	2216	2254	Freightliner	SX
4L97	Coatbridge	Felixstowe	2228	2230	SLK coal	SX
6S67	Healey Mills	Gartcosh	2237	2340		

Leith is an important railhead with a variety of commodities arriving both by *Speedlink* and also by private company trains. General goods are handled in VDA vans and large quantities of palletised fertilizer arrive from the Norsk Hydro terminal in Immingham. Steel pipes for use in domestic gas pipelines arrive from Hartlepool pipe mill, for coating. They are then despatched by rail to destinations such as St. Neots, Grimsby and Southampton. The Scottish Agricultural Industries (SAI) plant at Leith receives block trains of raw materials as follows: 6S41 - 0005 (MX) Haverton Hill-Leith (0608); 6B92 - 0624 (MX) Grangemouth-Leith (0812) and 6B96 - 0925

(WFO) Grangemouth-Leith (1142). Arrival times at Leith are shown in brackets. Other goods handled at Leith include grain from East Anglia and cars imported through the docks.

Bathgate has been much in the news since the reintroduction of a regular passenger service in 1986. It is the site of a large car distribution depot. Cars arrive from British Leyland plants and from Dover and Harwich. From Bathgate they are moved to showrooms all over Scotland. The rail services to Bathgate can be found detailed in the table on pages 120 and 121.

Grangemouth, near Falkirk is a *Railfreight* dedicated locomotive depot, which deals

Left: GRANGEMOUTH: On April 24 1986 Class 37 No. 37264 storms out of Grangemouth yard with 6D21, the Grangemouth-Mossend *Speedlink* service. During 1989, further modernisation at Grangemouth should provide a new locomotive servicing depot and *Speedlink* sidings on the site of the former steam shed. 6D21 continues to run in 1988; its traffic (as in 1986) is predominantly fuel oil for distribution to many parts of Scotland. *MR.*

EDINBURGH AREA TRIP FREIGHT SERVICES FROM AUGUST 1988
TIMES FROM MILLERHILL YARD

CODE	LOCO	TIME	TO (ARRIVAL TIME IN BRACKETS)	TRAFFIC	DAYS
B02	37	1042	Thornton (12.00 as 6G44), Rosyth (14.20), Millerhill (16.52)	Speedlink	SX
B03	37	0828	Bathgate (09.12), to work 4O38	cars	SX
B07	37	0630	Leith (06.55), Millerhill (07.55) Haymarket (09.12), Craigentinny (11.42), Millerhill (12.45)	Speedlink	SX
B08	26	0615	AFC instructions, priority to MGR	MGR	SuX
		1340	AFC instructions, priority to MGR	MGR	SX
B09	26	0625	AFC instructions, priority to MGR	MGR	SuX
B10	26	1235	AFC instructions, priority to MGR	MGR	SX
B11	08		Leith South Pillot	Speedlink	SuX
B12	08		Millerhill Yard Pilot	Speedlink	SuX
B21	08		Craigentinny pilot		all week
B22	08		Waverley pilot		all week
B23	08		Craigentinny CSD pilot		SuX
B24	37	1145	Haymarket CCD & Portobello CCD	Speedlink Coal	SX
B26	26	0610	AFC instructions, priority to MGR	MGR	SX
		1317	AFC instructions, priority to MGR	MGR	SX

The following diagrams also exist for departmental purposes:-

CODE	LOCO	TIME	TO (ARRIVAL TIME IN BRACKETS)	TRAFFIC	DAYS
B14	08		Slateford (ACE) pilot		SX
B15	37/0	0700	Millerhill ACE instructions		SuX
B16	37/0	0715	Engineers route train, Millerhill to Slateford, Inverkeithing or Thornton.		SuX
B17	2x37	2100	Millerhill ACE instructions		SO
B18	any	2200	Millerhill ACE instructions		SO
B19	any	2230	Millerhill ACE instructions		SO
B20	any	2300	Millerhill ACE instructions		SO
B25	any	2240	Millerhill ACE instructions		SO
B27	26	2050	Millerhill electrification instructions		all week
B28	26	2250	Millerhill electrification instructions		all week
B29	26	1030	Millerhill electrification instructions		SuX
B30	any	2100	Millerhill electrification instructions		SO
B31	47/4	2300	Millerhill ACE instructions		SX
B32	47/4	2110	Millerhill ACE instructions		SO
B33	2x20	2220	Millerhill electrification instructions		SuX

Left: BLINDWELLS: The B09 'trip' from Millerhill received instructions to carry two MGR trains of coal from Blindwells opencast site to Cockenzie power station, on March 1 1988. Class 26 No. 26007 prepares for the half mile dash along the ECML before reversing into the reception yard at Cockenzie. *MR.*

Right, upper: LEITH SOUTH: In glorious early morning sun Class 08 No. 08718 propels four tanks of anhydrous ammonia into the SAI factory at Leith. These arrived from Haverton Hill the previous evening. On March 1 1988, the yard contains, from left to right, fertilizer from Immingham, imported cars and empty pipe wagons awaiting a load of coated pipes for the south. *MR.*

predominantly with the petroleum traffic from the nearby BP refinery. The arrivals and departures at Grangemouth are listed in the table on page 123. Fuel oil from the refinery is distributed to every British Rail motive power depot in Scotland except Ayr, which is suppplied from Stanlow. In addition, the outlying fuel depots at Maxwelltown, Oban, Connel Ferry, Fort William, Inverness and Lairg receive fuel oil from Grangemouth via the *Speedlink* network.

Both Scotland's major airports are also rail-connected via Paisley Hawkhead oil depot and Prestwick oil terminal. The *Speedlink* yard at Grangemouth comprises just five sidings which cope more than adequately with the traffic generated by wagon loads of oil, the Blue Circle cement terminal and

Above: BATHGATE: A reminder of how rapidly the freight scene changes is provided by this view of Class 40 No. 40064 at Bathgate. On June 29 1980, it arrives at Bathgate with 4D64, the Millerhill-Mossend. Class 25 No. 25084 is shunting the 8J24 trip freight to Millerhill. In the last eight years both these locomotive classes have been withdrawn.

The direct freight only route to Airdrie has closed and a new passenger service to Bathgate has started. The signal box at Bathgate is no longer open but automotive traffic continues. The British Leyland vans seen here no longer travel from Bathgate but incoming cars continue to justify two full trainloads each day. *MR.*

GRANGEMOUTH FREIGHT FROM AUGUST 1988

CODE	LOCO	TIME	FROM	TO	TRAFFIC	DAYS
6B80		0245	Grangemouth Y	Oxwellmains	cement	TThSO
6D49		0300	Grangemouth O	Mossend	Speedlink	MX
6M34		0450	Grangemouth O	Dalston	oil	WSX
6B01		0531	Grangemouth O	Riccarton	oil	MO
6R42		0541	Grangemouth O	Prestwick	oil	MSX Y
6D79		0541	Grangemouth O	Hawkhead	oil	MSX Y/SO
6S92		0603	Grangemouth C	Leith	chemicals	SuX
6B92		0624	Grangemouth C	Leith	chemicals	MSX
N11	08	0655	Stirling pilot		Speedlink	SX
6D27		0705	Grangemouth O	Wishaw	oil	TO
N07	08	0720	Grangemouth Y	pilot	Speedlink	SX
N06	37	0830	Grangemouth	Mossend	LE	SX
		1002	Mossend	Stirling	Speedlink	SX
		1057	AFC instructions, shunt Cambus/Menstrie			SX
		1325	Stirling	Polmaise	Speedlink	SX
		1346	Polmaise	Plean	Speedlink	SX
		1415	Plean	Grangemouth Y	Speedlink	SX
6B96		0925	Grangemouth O	Leith	chemicals	WFO
6D26		1248	Grangemouth O	Mossend	Speedlink	SX
6N70		1351	Grangemouth O	Bishopbriggs	oil	SX
8X99		1707	Grangemouth C	Haverton Hill	chemicals	MO
6D21		1751	Grangemouth O	Mossend	Speedlink	SX
8X99		1835	Grangemouth C	Haverton Hill	chemicals	ThO
6V53		1858	Grangemouth C	Llandarcy	oil	MWO
6M38		1938	Grangemouth O	Carlisle Yard	oil	WSX
6E58		1956	Grangemouth O	Jarrow	oil	TWFO
6L51		2236	Grangemouth O	Leuchars	oil	MWO
6D22		2254	Grangemouth O	Mossend	Speedlink	SX

GRANGE MOUTH ARRIVALS - AUGUST 1988

CODE	LOCO	TIME	FROM	TO	TRAFFIC	DAYS
6N52		0039 Y	Oxwellmains		cement	TThSO
7N53		0039 Y	Mossend		Speedlink	MX
6S53		0335 O	Carlisle Yard		oil	MThX
6N24		0620 O	Leuchars		oil	TThO
7N51		0620 Y	Mossend		Speedlink	MX
6N67		0816 O	Hawkhead		oil	MO
6N63		1107 O	Bishopriggs		oil	MX
6N56		1129 C	Leith		chemicals	MX
6N59		1457 O	Wishaw		oil	TO
6S51		1612 C	Llandarcy		chemicals	WFO
6N55		1716 O	Hawkhead		oil	MSX Y
6S36		1742 O	Dalston		oil	WSX
6N61		1816 O	Riccarton		oil	MO
6S62		1856 O	Jarrow		oil	MWThO
6N58		1923 O	Leith		chemicals	WFO
8X98		2036 C	Haverton Hill		chemicals	TFO
7N69		2213 O	Mossend		Speedlink	SX

Key:- O = oil terminal
     C = B.P. chemicals
     Y = yard
     L = loco depot

the Russells distribution terminal (mainly bricks from Plymouth) at Grangemouth. The yard also stages traffic en route from Cambus, Stirling, Plean and Polmaise. In an attempt to further improve the *Railfreight* facilities at Grangemouth, a new traction maintenance depot and yard are to be constructed on the site of the old steam depot. Work on this project was planned to commence during 1989.

The ICI private siding at Larbert receives a twice-weekly block chemical train from Oakleigh. The return 'empties' run as 6M27, the 0631 departure on Saturdays and 6M27, the 1518 departure on Tuesdays.

North from Larbert there are *Speedlink* customers at Plean (Scottish Timber) and Polmaise (ARC). The Redland bricks and tiles company also utilizes *Railfreight* facilities at Plean.

DUNDEE & PERTH

RAILFREIGHT operations in Dundee centre on a collection of sidings to the west of the station on the north of the main line. The yard is used by both *Speedlink* traffic and the civil engineers department of British Rail. A yard pilot shunts in the Dundee area and this may be either a Class 08 locomotive or the larger Class 26. Steel traffic arrives from Scunthorpe and Teesside and bricks are handled at the Butterley Brick Company's private siding. The yard also acts as a staging point for cement traffic from Oxwellmains to the Blue Circle cement terminal at Camperdown Junction. Traffic arrives on 6A33, the

1738 Oxwellmains-Craiginches, and empty wagons are returned on 6B84, the 0040 Craiginches-Oxwellmains service.

A *Speedlink* 'trip' freight operates each day from Dundee yard to Montrose and Laurencekirk. The 7L21 service operates as required to terminals along the Aberdeen mainline and its crew are booked for an eight hour shift between 0700 and 1500. Agricultural lime arrives in Dundee from Thrislington on 6S92, the 1514 Scunthorpe-Guild Street *Speedlink* freight. From here it is taken to the sidings at Montrose and Laurencekirk. Return freight includes pota-

Above: GREENLOANING: In splendid evening sun on July 26 1988, Class 37 No. 37046 is photographed at Greenloaning, between Perth and Stirling. The 1845 Inverness-Mossend *Speedlink* (6D02) is running over two hours early on this occasion! A varied load includes empty cement wagons from Inverness to Oxwellmains and the empty bitumen tanks from Culloden Moor to Ellesmere Port, at the rear of the formation. *MR.*

Left: DUNDEE YARD: A busy scene at Dundee yard on July 28 1988 sees Class 26 No. 26021, the yard pilot, shunting out the 'cripples' from a rake of ballast wagons. On the left of the locomotive, the four PTA wagons also pictured below can be seen. They are waiting to join 6E89, the 1420 Aberdeen-Tyne Yard *Speedlink*. On the far left is Class 37 No. 37242, at the head of the 6M64 *Speedlink*. It will pick up VGA vans containing paper before continuing south, via a stop at Perth. *MR.*

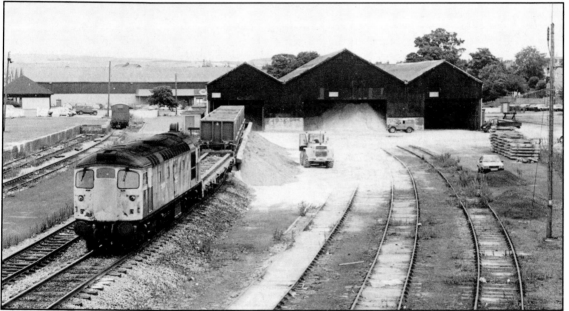

Above: MONTROSE: On July 28 1988, Class 26 No. 26015 stands in the goods yard at Montrose. Its load of four PTA lime tipplers have just discharged their load of limestone from County Durham. The locomotive will return to Dundee with the 7L22 'trip' working. *MR.*

toes from Montrose which run on a seasonal basis. A total of seven *Speedlink* services call at Dundee each 24 hours and these connect with wagons from the Laurencekirk trip as well as wagons of yarn, paper and whisky from Dundee freight depot.

Perth was once the site of a mechanised hump yard. This lay one and a half miles north of the station, on the Inverness route. Just a couple of sidings remained here in 1988 for use by the civil engineer.

The five daily *Speedlink* freights which call at Perth now attach and detach traffic in the station area or in the sidings to the south of the station. Local freight customers include the Dewars distillery at Inveralmond, Shell oil, and shippers of timber and lime.

A new traffic of gas oil from Grangemouth started in 1988, to Leuchars. The service supplies fuel for local military installations and is timetabled to arrive at Leuchars at 0130 on a TThO basis.

Above: DUNBLANE: A traffic flow which has ceased is that of bitumen from Ardrossan Harbour. On July 19 1984 the 1108 Inverness-Ardrossan 'empties' (7A61) are seen passing Dunblane behind Class 27 No. 27049. In 1988, this traffic travels from Ellesmere Port to Culloden Moor by *Speedlink* services. *PDS.*

Above: LAURENCEKIRK: On June 2 1988, Class 37 No. 37015 passes the yard at Laurencekirk with 6A19, the 0805 (SX) Mossend-Aberdeen *Speedlink* service. Class 37 No. 37198 stands in the yard headshunt, awaiting departure with the 7L22 trip freight to Dundee yard. On this occasion, the train comprised OTA and OBA wagons, containing timber. *David H. Allen.*

Above: BROUGHTY FERRY: The 1315 Aberdeen Guild Street-Willesden (6M64) is seen passing Broughty Ferry on July 28 1988. Class 37 No. 37242 is hauling timber from Elgin, Huntly and Inverurie, as well as the two *Freightliner* vehicles with government stores also pictured on page 128. *MR.*

Above: PERTH: Class 47 No. 47206 leaves Perth on June 22 1982 with 6B66, the afternoon *Speedlink* to Millerhill. In 1988, much of the city's *Speedlink* traffic is handled in the sidings south of the station. *PDS.*

ABERDEEN

SINCE July 25 1988 all freight traffic in the Aberdeen area has been marshalled at Aberdeen Guild Street, the site of the former *Freightliner* terminal. The concentration of all *Speedlink* traffic at Guild Street reduces trip working in the Aberdeen area as the majority of *Speedlink* customers utilize the sidings at Guild Street itself. A visit during July 1988 revealed a wide variety of traffics in the yard, including: Crosse & Blackwell products brought by road from Peterhead and bound for the south by rail, starch from Manchester Ardwick to local paper firms, coal from Yorkshire in J.G. Russell containers, paper for UK customers from Robertsbridge, and paper for Cognac in France from a local company.

The Waterloo branch to the north of the city was out of use in late 1988, although hopes are high that a new contract to move chemicals along the line may lead to its reopening. To the south of Aberdeen lies Craiginches yard. Whilst no longer used for *Speedlink* marshalling it contains three freight railheads and is still used by the civil engineer. On the Down side of the main line are sidings for fuel oil and agricultural lime

Above: ABERDEEN: Class 47 No. 47004 arrives in Aberdeen station with 6A32, the 1745 Elgin-Guild Street *Speedlink* service. On July 25 1988 the train comprised two *Freightliner* vehicles loaded with government stores. *MR.*

Above: INVERURIE: The yard at Inverurie remains busy with a variety of traffic. On July 26 1988, wagons from Greenock (molasses), Burngullow (china clay), Mossend (empty timber) and Thrislington (lime) were to be found in the sidings. Class 37 No. 37015 pauses at Inverurie with 6A22, the 0937 Elgin-Guild Street *Speedlink*. It deposited four empty timber wagons in the yard before continuing south with its train of government stores, carried in *Freightliner* containers. *MR.*

Left: ABERDEEN GUILD STREET - On July 25 1988, Guild Street goods depot became the main *Speedlink* yard for the north east of Scotland; it replaced Aberdeen Craiginches yard. On July 27 1988, Class 26 No. 26025 is the yard pilot because of the failure of the Class 08 locomotive normally allocated to this task. It has just arrived with the single TTA tank which is returning from Aberdeen Clayhills depot to Grangemouth. Behind the empty oil tank are three Norsk Hydro fertilizer vehicles which were tripped from J.G. Russell's siding at Ferryhill half-an-hour earlier. These wagons will be made up to form the overnight Speedlink service to Mossend yard (see table, below). *MR.*

ABERDEEN FREIGHT SERVICES FROM AUGUST 1988
TIMES AT GUILD STREET or CRAIGINCHES

CODE	LOCO	FROM	TO	ARR	DEP	TRAFFIC	DAYS
6B84		Craiginches	Oxwellmains		0040	cement	MX
6S63		Tees	Guild Street	04.36		Speedlink	MX
6A15		Guild Street	Elgin		0550	Speedlink	SX
A01	08	Guild Street	Craiginches/Russells		0625	Speedlink	SX
		Guild Street	Craiginches/Russells		1025	Speedlink	SX
		Guild Street	Craiginches/Russells		1405	Speedlink	SX
		Guild Street	Craiginches/Russells		1725	Speedlink	SX
		Guild Street	Craiginches		1920	Speedlink	SX
A03	37	Guild Street	Inverurie/		0942	Speedlink	SX
			Port Elphinstone				
		Guild Street	Clayhills/		1205	Speednk	SX
		Guild Street	Dyce/Inverurie		1402	Speedlink	SX
			Port Elphinstone				
A07	08	Aberdeen station pilot/shunt	Clayhills				daily
6S92		Scunthorpe	Guild Street	0823		Speedlink	SX
6A22		Elgin	Guild Street	1231		Speedlink	SX
6A19		Mossend	Guild Street	1317		Speedlink	MX
6M64		Guild Street	Willesden		1315	Speedlink	SX
6A27		Guild Street	Elgin		1337	Speedlink	SX
6E89		Guild Street	Tyne		1420	Speedlink	SX
6A32		Elgin	Guild Street	2039		Speedlink	SX
6O03		Guild Street	Mossend		2340	Speedlink	SX
6A33		Oxwellmains	Craiginches		2355	cement	SX

The following diagrams exist for departmental traffic:-

A02	47/4	Craiginches (0705)	ACE instructions				SX
A04	47/4	Craiginches (2040)	ACE instructions				SO
A06	47/4	Craiginches (2040)	ACE instructions				SO
A06	37	Craiginches (2045)					SO

whilst on the Up side there is a Blue Circle cement terminal served by a block load from Oxwellmains (see table). There is also a terminal for Clydesdale cement (Castle) which is not used at the moment but should see traffic at some stage during 1989, if plans to distribute cement from Gunnie near Motherwell are successful (see page 108).

Freight terminals to the north of Aberdeen are served by the A03 trip or one of the two daily *Speedlink* services to Elgin. At Elgin, the small goods depot handles a variety of traffic, the major commodity being timber. A recent service has started with containers carrying whisky or government stores. These travel to Aberdeen Guild Street from where

Above: INSCH: A summer downpour drenches Class 37 No. 37015 as it storms past Insch with 6A32, the 1755 Elgin-Craiginches *Speedlink* of June 2 1988. The service conveys a mixture of government stores and timber. *David H. Allen.*

they travel south on *Speedlink* services. Timber is also loaded at Keith, Huntly and Inverurie. The Chivas whisky distillery has private sidings at Keith and despatch whisky by rail to Dalmuir on a regular basis. At Inverurie there is a large goods yard from where lime from Thrislington and molasses from Greenock are unloaded. Wagons of china clay slurry en-route to Port Elphinstone are often stabled there as are OTA timber wagons awaiting timber. The timber traffic from the north east of Scotland is sent to a variety of customers with the paper mills at Irvine and Shotton taking the majority.

Right: PORT ELPHINSTONE is just over one mile south of Inverurie. Its paper works receives china clay from Cornwall, and despatches paper by *Speedlink* to Manchester and Glasgow. On July 26 1988, No. 47316 shunts at Port Elphinstone, having left its train, the Inverurie-Guild Street 'trip', (6A03) on the main line. After leaving three china clay tanks in the works, the engine picks up two loaded VDAs. Shunting proceeds rapidly as there is no 'lock in' facility and the train is blocking the single track to Dyce. *MR.*

Above: LAIRG is the northern outpost of the *Railfreight* empire in 1988. However, the introduction RETB signalling may well change this situation by enabling the operation of a night freight, carrying peat from Georgemas. On June 30 1987, Class 37 No. 37114 is picking up empty oil tanks at Lairg. These will return to Grangemouth with the first leg of their journey as 7H38, the 1400 (TFO) Lairg-Inverness *Speedlink*. *Don Gatehouse.*

INVERNESS, the capital of the Highlands is connected to the *Speedlink* network by a daily freight to Millerhill and a second daily service to Mossend. The yard at Millburn lies to the north of the mainline out of Inverness and acts as the focus for *Railfreight* activity in the north of Scotland. A single Class 08 shunting locomotive works as yard pilot and is reponsible for 'tripping' tanks of fuel oil to the nearby locomotive depot. It also 'trips' to the remains of the dock branch, where a new coal depot has been set up by J.G. Russell adjacent to the Far North line out of Inverness.

Fuel oil from Grangemouth may be bound for Lairg fuel depot (served on a Tuesday and Friday), Invergordon distillery (served each weekday) or the British Rail depot at Inverness. Towns north of Inverness no longer benefit from a general goods service since the withdrawal of the daily pick-up goods to Wick and Thurso in the early 1980s.

Grain is despatched from Muir of Ord on a seasonal basis and whisky from M.K. Shand travels by rail from Invergordon. This uses a single rail wagon which runs a continuous circuit from Invergordon to the Russell's container terminal at Gartcosh, (See page 109).

The grain terminal at Burghead and storage silos at Roseisle are both served by a conditional 'trip' service from Inverness.

This runs whenever there is traffic for the Burghead branch and leaves Inverness around midday. A second local company which benefits from rail connections is Highland Bitumen, at Culloden. Tanks of bitumen used for road resurfacing arrive from Ellesmere Port via the H11 'trip' (see table, overleaf). This 'trip' also carries timber on an occasional basis and may be extended to Carrbridge when necessary.

Between September and November 1988, the southern end of the Far North line was host to block trains conveying imported coal from Invergordon harbour to SSEB power stations.

An increase in *Railfreight* activity along the Far North line may be possible with the introduction of RETB signalling controlled by a single box at Dingwall. A night shift is very cheap to operate, as only one signalman's wages are needed to keep the whole line open. A trial run was made in Autumn

INVERNESS FREIGHT SERVICES FROM AUGUST 1988
TIMES AT INVERNESS YARD

CODE	LOCO	FROM	TO	ARR	DEP	TRAFFIC	DAYS
7H31		Mossend	Inverness			Speedlink	MX
H03	08	Inverness pilot, trip CCD/harbour				Speedlink	SX
H05	08	Inverness station pilot, shunt 6H25				Speedlink	SO
H06	08	Inverness station pilot					daily
7H27		Inverness	Invergordon		0718	Speedlink	MWTh
7H27		Inverness	Lairg		0718	Speedlink	TFO
H11	37	Inverness	Culloden		0800	Speedlink	SX
H12	37	Inverness	Burghead		1042	Speedlink	SX Y
6H25		Millerhill	Inverness	10.57		Speedlink	MX
7H28		Invergordon	Inverness	12.54		Speedlink	MWTh
6B68		Inverness	Millerhill		1340	Speedlink	SX
7H38		Lairg	Inverness	14.00		Speedlink	TFO
H13	37	Kyle of Lochalsh AFC instructions			1405	Speedlink	SX Y
6D02		Inverness	Mossend		1845	Speedlink	SX

The following diagrams exist for departmental traffic:-

H01	37/4	Georgemas (06.30) ACE instructions					TFO
H02	37	Inverness (07.35) ACE instructions					SX
H02	37	Inverness (06.45) ACE instructions					SX
H09	37	Inverness (20.30) ACE instructions					SO
H10	37	Inverness (20.40) ACE instructions					SO

Above: INVERNESS YARD: Class 08 No. 08717 returns to the east end of Millburn yard after depositing four PCA cement wagons in the Blue Circle cement terminal at Inverness. On July 17 1988, the yard also contained a variety of civil engineers vehicles and a rake of HEA hoppers carrying rock salt from Over and Wharton for use on Scottish roads in winter. *MR.*

Right: BURGHEAD: Class 47 No. 47210 runs round its train of grain from East Anglia before reversing it into the unloading shed at Burghead, on June 3 1988. The train is 6H12, the 1040 (SX Y) from Inverness. *David H. Allen.*

1988, of a train conveying peat from the Far North line to a consignee in Leicestershire, and at the time of going to press we were awaiting the outcome with interest.

Left: CULLODEN MOOR: The 6H11 'trip' from Inverness arrives at Culloden on July 27 1988. No. 37262 pauses in the old station as the guard (out of sight) releases the ground frame controlling the entrance to the Highland bitumen sidings. The first three wagons carry timber to Carrbridge; the remainder are TTAs conveying bitumen from Ellesmere Port. *MR.*

Below: INVERGORDON: On August 13 1981, the daily Inverness-Wick/Thurso service passes Invergordon station behind No. 26036. The first five wagons contain fuel oil from Grangemouth refinery for the BP depot at Lairg. This still receives a twice weekly train in 1988. The last vehicle, a VVV van is from Newark to Thurso and carries electrical goods for the Currys retail outlet in Thurso. *PDS.*

Above: INVERGORDON: The guard of 7H27, the 0718 (MWThO) Inverness-Invergordon *Speedlink* service watches as the train sets back into the sidings at Invergordon distillery, on June 29 1987. Class 37 No. 37421 is in superb condition after working the royal train to Invergordon a few days earlier. The train comprises a whisky tank, to be loaded for Gartcosh and three OBAs which will pick up timber at Muir of Ord. *Don Gatehouse.*

THE WEST HIGHLANDS

Above: LOCHABER: On August 17 1984, the YO2 'trip' is seen shunting at Lochaber. Class 20 No. 20049 is propelling wagons of bauxite into the plant. On the right, the end of an OCA wagon can just be seen; this will be loaded with aluminium ingots for the West Midlands. *David H. Allen.*

THE West Highland routes to Oban, Fort William and Mallaig are well known for their dramatic scenery. Less well appreciated is the considerable tonnage of freight traffic to be seen along these lines. Fort William is the site of a British Aluminium smelter. The Lochaber plant generates a large amount of rail traffic. Ninety thousand tons of bauxite arrive each year from Blyth and finished aluminium ingots are despatched by rail to Cardiff and Mossend yard. The Cardiff traffic travels on *Freightliner* vehicles in a *Speedlink* service as far as Coatbridge *Freightliner* terminal, from where it proceeds south on the regular Coatbridge to Pengam *Freightliner* service. Aluminium in *Speedlink* wagons is sent to steel terminals in the West Midlands via Mossend yard.

Three miles out of Fort William, on the Mallaig line, is the Corpach paper mill. China clay from Pontsmill in Cornwall is rail delivered as are wood pulp from Aberdeen and oil from Grangemouth. Finished paper is sent in Speedlink wagons to Pensnett, Wolverton and elsewhere whilst paper to Cardiff again utilises the *Freightliner* service from Coatbridge. *Freightliner* vehicles loaded with paper travel on *Speedlink* services from Corpach to Coatbridge.

Fuel oil to Fort William, Corpach, Connel Ferry and Oban is delivered by rail from Grangemouth refinery. This traffic travels via the daily Grangemouth to Mossend *Speedlink* freights and the daily West Highland *Speedlink* services (see table). Fuel tanks to Mallaig and the second oil terminal at Oban travel from Bowling. Here, the oil storage facilities are supplied by coastal shipping and forward fuel oil to both Oban and Mallaig. Oil to Mallaig must travel on 2Y55, the 1610 Fort William -Mallaig passenger service. The empty tanks return on 2Y58, the 1845 Mallaig-Fort William train. In order to travel with the passenger service, oil must be conveyed in wagons equipped with a vacuum brake. The inclusion of revenue earning freight vehicles in a passenger service is unique to the Mallaig line.

Timber is loaded at several locations in the West Highlands with regular consignments forwarded from Arrochar, Ardlui, Crianlarich Lower, Taynuilt and Fort

William. The two major destinations for this traffic are the paper mills at Shotton and Irvine.

The introduction of RETB signalling along the West Highland route may allow further timber traffic to be loaded at sites along the main line. The economy of night time operation means that a freight train may occupy the main line for long periods overnight, thereby eliminating any interruptions to the daily passenger timetable. Similar resignalling in Caithness has allowed *Railfreight* to forward peat from Scotscalder, by parking a freight train on the main line overnight to avoid disruption of the regular passenger service.

FORT WILLIAM FREIGHT SERVICES, FROM AUGUST 1988.

CODE	LOCO	FROM	TO	MALLAIG JCT YD		TRAFFIC	DAYS
				ARR	DEP		
7Y31		Mossend	Mallaig Junc	0059		Speedlink	MX
6D03		Fort William	Mossend	0215	0239	Alumina	MX
6Y35		Mossend	Fort William	0529	0556	Alumina	MX
YO2	20	Mallaig Junc	Fort William Station			Speedlink	SX
			British Alcan			Speedlink	SX
			West Highland Oil			Speedlink	SX
			Corpach			Speedlink	SX
7D19		Corpach	Mossend	1159	1219	Speedlink	SX
7Y37		Mossend	Corpach	1818	1852	Speedlink	SX
7D10		Corpach	Mossend	1850	1910	Speedlink	SX

The following diagram exists for departmental traffic:-

YO1	37/4	Fort William (0755) ACE instructions					TWX

Above: OBAN: Awaiting departure from Oban on June 25 1986 is Class 37 No. 37051, in charge of the 7D09 *Speedlink* service to Mossend. *Don Gatehouse.*

Left: BANAVIE: On June 23 1986, No. 37408 departs from Banavie, amidst the spectacular characteristic scenery of the West Highlands, with the 1605 Fort William-Mallaig passenger service. Note the three fuel tankers attached to the rear of the four-coach formation (See also text, page 134). *Don Gatehouse.*

Right: FORT WILLIAM (OIL): The West Highland Oils company has a small private yard at Fort William, which receives oil from Grangemouth. On August 16 1984, Class 20 No. 20049 shunts fuel tanks at the yard as part of its daily work on the Y02 'trip' diagram. *David H. Allen.*

Left, upper: MALLAIG JUNCTION: Mallaig Junction yard at Fort William contains nine sidings, of which seven are used for *Speedlink* traffic. On August 16 1984, Class 37 No. 37039 sets back into the yard with 7B05, the 1330 Mossend-Corpach duty. Fuel oil from Grangemouth to Corpach fills the five TTA tanks at the front of the train whilst the next four wagons are PRAs containing china clay from Pontsmill to Corpach. In 1988, this freight runs as 7Y37 and arrives at Mallaig Junction at 1818. *David H. Allen.*

Left, lower: DUMBARTON CENTRAL: Class 37 No. 37412 enters the Down loop at Dumbarton Central station whilst working 7Y41, the 0945 (TThO) Mossend-Arrochar *Speedlink* 'trip', on July 14 1988. Normally, 7Y41 conveys empty timber wagons to Arrochar, but on this occasion the only traffic was government stores to Glen Douglas. *PDS.*